JESUS
NOW

JESUS NOW

UNVEILING THE PRESENT-DAY MINISTRY OF CHRIST

FRANK VIOLA

David C Cook

transforming lives together

JESUS NOW
Published by David C Cook
4050 Lee Vance View
Colorado Springs, CO 80918 U.S.A.

David C Cook Distribution Canada
55 Woodslee Avenue, Paris, Ontario, Canada N3L 3E5

David C Cook U.K., Kingsway Communications
Eastbourne, East Sussex BN23 6NT, England

LCCN 2014933915
ISBN 978-0-7814-0591-1
eISBN 978-0-7814-1129-5

© 2014 Frank Viola
Published in association with the literary agency of
Daniel Literary Group, Nashville, TN 37215.

The Team: Alex Field, Karen Lee-Thorp, Amy Konyndyk,
Nick Lee, Caitlyn Carlson, Karen Athen
Cover Design: Nick Lee
Printed in the United States of America
First Edition 2014

1 2 3 4 5 6 7 8 9 10

022614

To Leonard Sweet:
friend, colleague, interpreter of symbols,
and seer of that which is to come.

CONTENTS

THE PROVENANCE OF ORDINARY THINGS

Everything in life has a backstory. The French word *provenir* means "a coming forth from, a chronology, or lineage."

It even implies custody, a history of ownership or belonging. As a noun, it suggests there is a backstory for something we hold dear, a primal origin or a source. The word is used most typically in our culture for the his(story) of an artifact or antique.

We as Christians have a backstory too, one that tells of our source of life and our lineage as people of God—an extraordinary lineage of grace and wonder.

You see, whenever you attach a story to something, you turn an ordinary thing into an extraordinary gift of sacred blessing. Stories are the seeds of human existence. In them are contained the DNA of our identity. When we embrace them, nourish them, feed them, own them, we discover who we are. And through them, we are encouraged to bloom into the beautiful flora we were designed to be. Our tales are our talismans; our imaginations, our keys to the Scriptures.

In *Jesus Now*, Frank Viola invites you to use your imagination to take part in a journey that will lead you into an extraordinary new world where you can discover Jesus in present tense, living color. In doing so, you will discover the stories that reveal who you are.

One of the most famous all-night conversations in history took place between C. S. Lewis and J. R. R. Tolkien. From dusk to dawn, they discussed the meaning of fire and fable, sacred and secular, story and myth, legend and fairy tale.

The morning dawned with Lewis persuaded by Tolkien that "the story of Christ is simply a true myth: a myth working on us in the same way as the others, but with this tremendous difference that [the Christ story] really happened."

Based on this conversation, these two literary giants divided up the narrative landscape between them: Lewis tumbled us through a wardrobe into an alternate world of faith; Tolkien vaulted us into an alternate world of fantasy. The world was never the same.

All history is God's love story. There is no event in space or time unrelated to the Jesus story, and there is no metaphor in existence unrelated to Jesus. "All roads lead to Rome" was the brag of the ancient Romans. "All metaphors lead to Jesus" is the vaunt and jaunt of the Christian life.

Provenance tells the story behind, with, and under the story. Provenance is proof that people heard and experienced the story encased in an ordinary object. Provenance elevates and authenticates the story.

Most Christians know the story of what Jesus did when He was on earth. But the part of the Jesus story that's rarely told is about what He is doing *now*—between the ascension and the second coming.

Frank Viola is a master at the discipline of historical context, and *Jesus Now* is a masterpiece that shows us how to "Christify" our story—to move from an unscripted spirituality to a scripturally scripted identity.

You are a story wrapped in skin. In every nook and cranny, around every bend and corner of your life, is a story awaiting you to bring it from potential to kinetic form. At a time when so many Christian stories have never been Christified, shaped by the plotline of Christ, and infused by the presence of His Spirit, Jesus Now comes as a godsend.

Until Jesus, we were on opposite sides of the divide between the divine and human. Why so many Christians have such trouble speaking well of the bridge that carries us across this divide is more of a mystery than ever after reading every one of Viola's books, especially this one.

When I finished Frank's penetrating exegesis of the meta-phors of Jesus' present-day ministry, the conviction hit me in the heart: giving Jesus' life, death, and resurrection provenance in the twenty-first century is our mission. *Jesus Now* reveals how we are the provenance of the Jesus story.

This book will show you how to write the gospel within the text and textures of your own life. *Jesus Now* stands as a challenge for each of us to move from numbers to narratives, from scorecards to storyboards, to have our lives become an ongoing provenance for the Jesus story, based on the authentics of the gospel.

Sigmund Freud tells the story of a three-year-old boy whom he heard calling out from a dark room in the night. "Auntie," the boy cried, "talk to me! I'm frightened because it is so dark."

His aunt answered him from another room: "What good would that do? You can't see me."

"That doesn't matter," replied the child. "When you talk, it gets light."

When you talk, does it get light? Is your life an authentic provenance for the Jesus story?

Each of us contains the Jesus story in the heart of our very beings. Jesus is our provenance. And for us to see that, the Scriptures are our true authentics.

To grow as a disciple in Christ is to link our unique story to the provenance of Jesus. Frank's book helps us find our provenance, that storyline in our hearts that becomes our authentic Bibline to Jesus. Through the threads of Frank Viola's storytelling, we can discover our authentic lineage as people of Christ—and embrace His incarnational provenance, the story in our hearts that makes everyday things shine with the silvery light of God.

We can treat the scriptural stories of Jesus like a mere antique collection of silverware, trotted out here and there for display. Or we can cherish, use, and honor each piece and morsel with family time around the table to connect to our divine heritage through the stories of our faith.

This is a book that uses the silverware of Scripture to serve up an extraordinary feast. Each metaphor in this book that points to Christ's present-day ministry will give you a taste of God's tremendous love and grace and will impress upon your soul memories of delectable delight.

The story of Jesus—past and present—is the food of discipleship. Taste and see.

Leonard Sweet
E. Stanley Jones Chair in Evangelism, Drew University
Distinguished Visiting Professor, George Fox University

WHAT IS JESUS DOING NOW?

There's a lovely little story about a skydiver who drifted over a hundred miles off course and landed in a dense forest. Strung up in the tree, tangled, and terrified of the fast-approaching night, he began to yell out for help. After a few minutes, a man who was out for a walk chanced upon the skydiver.

"Hello! I need help! Where am I?" called the man in the tree.

"You're stuck in a tree, with no way out. You're surrounded by a forest, and it's getting dark," the other man replied.

"Of all my luck," said the skydiver to him, "I get stuck with a minister as a rescuer!"

Hearing this, the passerby wondered aloud how the distressed man knew about his occupation as a religious teacher.

"Well," the man in the tree said, "I just assumed you must be a minister, as what you've said is both utterly true and absolutely useless in helping me."

When professional ministers hear this story, they usually get a chuckle out of it—in part because they can detect the grain of truth it holds. So much of our conversations about spiritual things, while perhaps good and even spot-on, are nearly devoid of relevant impact. It's not only Christianity that gets targeted by this critique—most academic or philosophical movements also struggle to reach us where we really live.

One of the greatest concerns I have for the "good news" today is that we often present a gospel that is more true than useful. This is never more true than when we're considering the subject and actor of our entire faith: Jesus Christ.

Think about it: The story is familiar to all Christians. The Gospels introduce us to the earthly ministry of Jesus. He was born in Bethlehem. He grew up in the ill-starred town of Nazareth, where He labored as an artisan. Around age thirty He was baptized in the Jordan River by John the Baptist, and He began His ministry.

Interestingly, Jesus' ministry lasted less than four years. He was crucified outside the city of Jerusalem, rose again from the dead three days later, and spent forty days on earth in His resurrected state. He then ascended into heaven, taking His seat at the right hand of God the Father.

In our book *Jesus: A Theography*, Leonard Sweet and I retold the incredible story of Jesus' earthly ministry, using all the biblical material from Genesis to Revelation. We also discussed in some detail His preexistent state before creation and His promised second coming at the end of the age.

To my knowledge, few books have been dedicated to exploring the present-day ministry of Jesus. By "present-day ministry," I'm referring to what Jesus has been doing since His ascension and will continue to do until His second coming.

Herein lies the aim of this book. It's an exploration into the present-day ministry of Christ. And it seeks to answer the question, *what is Jesus Christ doing right now, and how is His present-day ministry useful to me?*

As we reflect on the Lord's earthly ministry, the following aspects stand out:

> He preached the gospel of the kingdom.
> He revealed His Father.
> He healed the sick.
> He performed miracles.
> He cast out demons.
> He fed the poor.
> He befriended sinners.
> He rebuked the religious.
> He trained and sent disciples.

He went to the cross and dealt with the effects
of the fall.
He rose from the dead, ushering in the new
creation and becoming Lord of the world.

The Lord then ascended into heaven to take His place of authority and power. Yet Jesus Christ isn't sitting at the Father's right hand passively waiting to return to planet Earth. No, He is still active today. And the Man in the glory has a very specific ministry.

Concerning His personality, plan, and purpose, Jesus is "the same yesterday and today and forever" (Heb. 13:8). Concerning His ministry, however, it has changed somewhat from "the days of His flesh" (Heb. 5:7).

In this book we will explore the different aspects of the present-day ministry of Christ. We will find out what Jesus is doing now and its relevance to you and me.

Yesterday in Hebrews 13:8 has in view Christ's ministry before creation as well as His earthly ministry. *Today* has in view His present-day ministry. *Forever* has in view His ministry that moves into eternity.

Our focus in this book will be upon Jesus Christ's ministry today. Or to put it succinctly, *Jesus now*.

Let's begin …

THERE'S A MAN IN THE GLORY

There's a Man in the glory
Whose Life is for me.
He's pure and He's holy,
Triumphant and free.
He's wise and He's loving,
How tender is He!
His Life in the glory,
My life must be;
His Life in the glory,
My life must be.

There's a Man in the glory
Whose life is for me.
He overcame Satan;
From bondage He's free.
In Life He is reigning;
How kingly is He!
His Life in the glory,
My life must be;
His Life in the glory,
My life must be.

There's a Man in the glory
Whose Life is for me.
In Him is no sickness;
No weakness has He.
He's strong and in vigor,
How buoyant is He!
His Life in the glory
My life may be;
His Life in the glory,
My life may be.

There's a Man in the glory
Whose Life is for me.
His peace is abiding;
How patient is He!
He's joyful and radiant,
Expecting to see
His Life in the glory
Lived out in me;
His Life in the glory
Lived out in me.

—Mary E. McDonough, 1787

CHAPTER 1

GREAT HIGH PRIEST

Therefore, since we have a great high priest who has passed through the heavens, Jesus the Son of God, let us hold fast our confession.

Hebrews 4:14

When I think of Jesus as our high priest, I'm reminded of a story I once heard about several generations of holy men who lived outside a particular village near a mighty river. During the lifetime of one holy man, the river overflowed its bounds, exposing the village to grave danger.

The women and men came to the priest and asked him to pray to God to save them, and so he did. He stole away to a secret place, where he uttered the sacred words and asked the Lord for His favor. Miraculously the town was saved. As long as he was alive, the village remained untouched.

But eventually the holy man died, and once again the river threatened to flood the town. The elders came to the priest's apprentice and begged him to go before God on their behalf. So, with fear and trembling, this holy man took it upon himself to seek God's favor. But he had forgotten where the secret place was. He came before the Lord and said the sacred words, then he prayed, "Oh God, You are not a small and petty territorial divinity. The heavens are Your throne room, and the whole earth is Your footstool! What need have You for secret places? But please accept these words as a gift offering, and if You see fit, spare this town."

And the Lord did just that. The town was spared. As long as the great man was alive, the town was safe. But then he died, and once more the village was thrown into peril. The town leaders sought out the student of the last holy man and asked him to do what his predecessors had done before him. The only problem was that he had forgotten both the secret place and the sacred words. And so he simply came into God's presence and whispered to the Most High, "Lord, You are not to be found in any one spot on this earth, or even in special words—for You are more profound than any single word could ever hope to describe. So I pray that You will hear these common words. Still the waters of the river and save the village!" And God's hand was moved. The town was saved.

But this holy man also grew old and died, and one day his own heir was called on to come before God on behalf of the village. This priest was, however, a poor one. He did not know the secret place or the sacred words. In fact, he didn't particularly believe in miracles. So when the villagers approached him, he simply stared at them, not saying a word.

At last he stood up, grabbed his coat and work gloves, and said to the dumbstruck villagers, "Come on! We have a lot of work to do. We must *move* the village to higher ground!" As they left the priest's home, two unseen figures came out of the shadows—God and one of His angels.

God smiled and nodded in the direction in which the men had just gone in. "This last one's my favorite, you know," God said. "He's most like Me, actually. He did what none of the others could. They all said special words and invested energy in certain places. But this one—he *joined* me in my work. Instead of just talking about change, he cared enough to be the change!"

I love this simple little story. God is more concerned about loving people practically than about simply investing in a series of rituals. This is the context from which we must consider Jesus Christ, our real high priest. He is the one who rolls up His sleeves and joins us in the broken places of our lives. The role of high priest is as infinitely practical from this vantage point.

In order to understand Jesus' ministry as our great high priest, we need to review the role of the high priest in the Old Testament.

Essentially, Israel's high priest represented God before the people and the people before God. This was a functional role initially. It was meant to be a practical transaction between the high priest and God on behalf of the people.

Once a year, the high priest would enter the Most Holy Place in the temple of God to offer the blood of innocent animals. The blood of those animals would cover the sins of the people for an entire year.

Having made a sacrifice for himself first and then for the people, the high priest would bring the blood of animals into the Most Holy Place and sprinkle it on the mercy seat, which was understood to be God's throne.

However, even though the blood of animals covered the sins of God's people, it could not remove the root of sin. Nor could it cleanse the consciences of the people. Israel still struggled with guilt and a sense of condemnation.

The book of Hebrews spills a great deal of ink in presenting Jesus Christ as our great high priest—the fulfillment of the Old Testament high priest, who was a type and a shadow of Jesus.

In fact, the book of Hebrews is built around the theme of the Lord's present-day ministry as high priest. This is often missed because there are five parenthetical warnings in Hebrews that break up the author's flow of thought. Those warnings are found in the following texts:

> Hebrews 2:1–4
> Hebrews 3:7–4:13
> Hebrews 5:11–6:20
> Hebrews 10:26–39
> Hebrews 12:15–29

If you read the book of Hebrews without these warnings, you will get a clear and uninterrupted presentation of the high-priestly ministry of Christ from beginning to end.

A Greater High Priest

Unlike the Old Testament high priest, who had to enter the Most Holy Place each year to atone for the nation's sin through the shedding of animal blood, Jesus Christ entered the Most Holy Place in heaven *once and for all* with His own blood.

By this sacrificial act, Jesus obtained eternal redemption for us (Heb. 9:12–28).

But that's not all.

Not only did Jesus forgive all our sins—past, present, and future transgressions—through His shed blood, but on the cross He also destroyed the power of sin:

> Knowing this, that our old self was cruci-
> fied with Him, in order that our body of sin
> might be done away with, so that we would
> no longer be slaves to sin; for he who has died
> is freed from sin. (Rom. 6:6–7)

Beyond that, the blood of Christ—having satisfied God's holiness—cleanses our consciences, removes our guilt, annihilates our shame, and takes away our sense of condemnation.

All of these things make the new covenant much more powerful than the old covenant.

A Better Covenant

It is my observation that many Christians today live like old-covenant people rather than new-covenant people. According to Hebrews, the new covenant is far superior to the old (8:6). This is because Jesus is greater than any other priest. Thus He is called our "great high priest" (4:14).

Consider the tight relationship that Abraham, Moses, and David had with God. The author of Hebrews made a pretty remarkable statement in this regard. He said that those who are under the new covenant have a closer relationship with God than our spiritual forefathers:

> And all these [people], having gained approval
> through their faith, did not receive what was
> promised, because God had provided some-
> thing better for us, so that apart from us they
> would not be made perfect. (Heb. 11:39–40)

Is your relationship with the Lord closer and more glorious than that of Abraham, Moses, and David? If not, then you— like many other believers—are living like an Old Testament Israelite when God has given you His new covenant sealed with the blood of His precious Son.

In other words, you are living far below your potential and what God desires for you.

A Cleansed Conscience

It is the presence of sin in our consciences that hinders the unrestricted communion we can enjoy with God. But the high-priestly ministry of Jesus cleanses our consciences. This means that the blood of Christ removes the guilt, shame, and condemnation that so often debilitate us.

The author of Hebrews argued that the blood of bulls and goats could never remove the consciousness of sins from God's people (Heb. 10:2). This means that even though the Old Testament high priest shed the blood of goats and bulls to cover the sins of the people, the people were always conscious of their own sinfulness. Their guilt remained. Their consciences still condemned them.

By contrast, the blood of Jesus removes the sin consciousness from our minds, giving us a pure and clean conscience, making us feel as though we've never sinned (Heb. 9:1–14; 10:1–22).

How can this be? It's because the blood of Christ was enough to satisfy God. It was enough to forgive you and me. And when God forgives, He forgets. The author of Hebrews stated twice that part of the new covenant is that God "will remember their sins no more" (8:12; see also 10:17).

Consequently, the only people on this earth who should never feel guilty are Christians. We'll discuss this in depth later in the book.

Accepted in the Beloved

I think it's important that we be constantly reminded that in Jesus Christ, God accepts us as we are—fully and completely. Therefore, it is a mistake to measure God's acceptance by your circumstances or even your deeds. So many Christians are stuck on the treadmill of religious performance. They set their conduct up as the basis for their standing with God.

If you tune in to Christian television or radio, a large percentage of modern-day preachers are presenting a gospel of condemnation. Their message can be boiled down to the following: "You have to do better to make God happy." In our own strength, from our own energies, we must "work out" our salvation with a great deal of "fear and trembling" (Phil. 2:12). It's a backbreaking kind of labor that's called for.

This gives birth to what I call the Phantom Christian Syndrome. The Phantom Christian is the imaginary self to which you compare yourself. You look at the Phantom Christian and think to yourself, *Someday I'll be this way. I'm going to try harder to be a good Christian.*

Get clear on this. We approach Christ daily the same way we did on the first day of our faith journey: totally helpless in our own efforts, in need of a Savior to be the One to heal and carry us. Colossians 2:6 says it best: "Just as you received Christ Jesus as your Lord, so also you must continue to follow Him" (NLT). Because of the truth that He is the same yesterday, today, and forever, we are always in the same posture—in absolute need of His grace and work in our hearts. We never move beyond that point. It is only by the shed blood of Christ that we stand in the absolute sinless perfection of Christ Himself. Through His blood, the perfections of Jesus are afforded to us.

The blood of Christ was enough to satisfy God's holy justice, wasn't it? It was enough to satisfy His demands, right? The issue, then, is settled forever. The perfection of the Lord flows on your behalf. Jesus stands as the spotless Lamb of God for you to God and for God to you.

So if you have repented and trusted in Christ, right now you stand in His perfection.

This is a gift. You've done nothing to earn it. If you choose to stand in yourself, you will continue to have a condemned conscience. The Phantom Christian will emerge to accuse you, and you'll crawl right back on the religious performance treadmill.

Your acceptance before a holy God is not a question of effort or attainment. It's a question of what Christ has done. By Christ's blood that was shed for you, God has made peace with you.

Thus approaching God should never be based on your attainments or on your works—whether good or bad. *It is always based solely on the blood of Christ.*

Put another way, your righteousness is not based on your work but on the work of another. For this reason, you can do nothing to make yourself more acceptable to God over and above what Jesus, your high priest, has already done for you at Calvary.

You cannot add to it, and you cannot take away from it.

The Way into the Holiest

Our acceptance is never based on our works or our outward condition. It's always and forever based on the finished work of Christ. And that work is final and complete.

> Therefore, brethren, since we have confidence
> to enter the holy place by the blood of Jesus, by
> a new and living way which He inaugurated for
> us through the veil, that is, His flesh, and since
> we have a great priest over the house of God, let
> us draw near with a sincere heart in full assur-
> ance of faith, having our hearts sprinkled clean
> from an evil conscience and our bodies washed
> with pure water. (Heb. 10:19–22)

Consequently, you and I have perpetual access to the throne of God on the basis of the blood. Jesus Christ is your acceptance. God has accepted you in the Beloved (Eph. 1:6 KJV). He has placed you in Christ.

The favor of God rests exclusively upon His own Son. *But the good news of the gospel is that you have been placed in Christ.*

Satan's chief attack, then, is to unseat your position in Christ. It's to get you to question your acceptance and your right standing with God. It's to accuse you and put you back under guilt and condemnation.

The idea that you must do something in yourself to obtain God's love and acceptance bears all the hallmarks of the Devil.

His major weapon is accusation. His name—*Devil*—means "slanderer or accuser." The nature of our Enemy is to slander, defame, and accuse us and other believers.

The remedy for his spiritual assault is to arm yourself with a clean conscience through the blood of Christ. The blood is the divine weapon against the fiery accusations of Satan.

But there must come a point in your Christian life where you believe and accept the value and meaning of the blood as God sees it. You must come to a point where you believe that Christ's blood completely satisfies God's requirements. Through the finished work of Jesus on the cross, your acceptance by God is absolute and unconditional.

Spiritual maturity and pleasing God are different matters, however, and we will get to those subjects in another chapter. But please understand: You don't serve God to get God's favor and acceptance. You serve God from the basis of having His favor and acceptance. And there's a world of difference between those two things.

Consequently, the basis of our acceptance is the finished work of Christ (Heb. 10:19; 1 John 1:7); the sphere of our acceptance is being in Christ (2 Cor. 5:21; Eph. 1:6–7); and the peace of our acceptance is our standing in God's grace by faith (Rom. 3:25; 5:1–2; Eph. 6:13–14).

The greatest weapon we can wield against the Devil is a fresh apprehension of the absolute satisfaction of God the Father in His Son on our behalf. This is the way of deliverance from condemnation (Rom. 8:31–34).

So the ultimate question is, whom will you side with—your accuser or your advocate?

God answers the accuser by the blood of His Son. So look away from yourself and look to your high priest. Your victory over the Enemy lies there.

The Finger or the Hand?

Lest you be confused, there is an important difference between the illumination of the Holy Spirit and the accusation of the Enemy.

I call it the difference between the finger and the hand.

Let me explain.

One way Satan accuses us is in our consciences, overwhelming us with a sense of condemnation and unworthiness to the point of hopelessness and even despair.

Again, standing in the virtue of the blood of Christ is the remedy for the Enemy's accusations.

> They triumphed over him by the blood of the Lamb. (Rev. 12:11 NIV)

The blood of Christ looms larger in God's eyes than any sin you or I could ever commit.

Thus one of Satan's foremost weapons is the sense of accusation, which obstructs our fellowship with God. Accusation causes us to withdraw from the "throne of grace" instead of "boldly" coming to it as Hebrews exhorts (4:16 KJV).

By contrast, when the Holy Spirit enlightens and illuminates us, He points to a *specific issue* in our lives that we need to repent of or deal with in His light.

Like the finger, the Spirit's illumination is very specific. And it always leads us to Christ.

When the Enemy accuses, it's often a vague sense of guilt, condemnation, and unworthiness.

Like the hand, it's unspecific.

Learning to distinguish between the finger and the hand—the Spirit's enlightenment and the Enemy's accusation—keeps us from being debilitated by the paralysis of self-analysis.

The key to making progress in the spiritual path is to keep your focus on Christ rather than on yourself.

Stand in the virtue of the shed blood of Jesus—the only thing that makes us worthy to come before our Father, who is pure holiness and light.

Neither your sin nor your stupidity prevent God from accepting you, loving you, and forgiving you.

As A. W. Tozer once said about the Lord Jesus, "He knows the worst about you and is the One who loves you the most."[1]

If that's not good news, I don't know what is.

---

1   A. W. Tozer, *And He Dwelt among Us* (Ventura, CA: Regal, 2009), 136.

A Misguided Teaching

Most errors circulating in the Christian world today can be found in the New Testament era. In particular, the two main enemies of the gospel—legalism and libertinism (license to sin)—were both present in the early church.

Galatians was written to legalists—hence the strong emphasis on liberty, freedom, and grace. James was written to libertines, those who presumed on the grace of God and turned it into a license to sin. Thus the book of James is strong on obedience, faith that expresses itself in works, repentance (for the believer), and false faith (or presumption).

The grace of God that is envisioned in the New Testament is amazing, radical, and beyond belief. However, in their reaction to legalism, some Christians have distorted the grace of God into a license for sinning. Interestingly, this same thing was happening in the first century:

> Certain individuals … have secretly slipped in among you. They are ungodly people, who pervert the grace of our God into a license for immorality and deny Jesus Christ our only Sovereign and Lord. (Jude v. 4 NIV)

Many years ago I was part of a new church plant where most
of the members came out of a religion-based, duty-based, law-
based form of Christianity. The person who planted the church
was strong on "radical grace." However, there was no balance in
his message, and he ended up ignoring many New Testament
texts that show us that God's grace is not a license to sin but
rather an empowering force that teaches us to defeat sin:

> For the grace of God has appeared that offers
> salvation to all people. It teaches us to say "No"
> to ungodliness and worldly passions, and to
> live self-controlled, upright and godly lives in
> this present age. (Titus 2:11–12 NIV)

The result was that licentiousness broke out everywhere in
the church. People would flaunt and even evangelize their sin
under the banners "we are free in Christ" and "we're under
grace, not law."

Point: if you're preaching grace, and immorality breaks out
everywhere you preach, then you're not preaching grace. You're
preaching something else.

As I've pointed out in my book *Revise Us Again*, the three
gospels that were present in the first-century church are still
with us today: the gospel of legalism, the gospel of libertinism,
and the gospel of lordship and liberty (which is the gospel that

both Jesus and Paul preached). I talk more about these three gospels in chapter 7.

That said, some erroneously teach that because Christians are under grace, all the "hard sayings" of Jesus about taking up your cross, bearing the cross, and so on, don't apply to us today. In fact, some go so far as to say that *all* of Jesus' teachings before the cross do not apply to new covenant believers.

But this teaching is simply false. With the exception of those statements by Jesus that were locally rooted in Jewish first-century culture, the bulk of Jesus' teachings have direct application for us today. In fact, those teachings are reiterated throughout the New Testament epistles and Revelation.

I'm a strong proponent of the idea that because of the blood of Christ and its power, Christians don't have to feel guilty. And we are free from condemnation.

However, if a Christian sins against another person, or the Lord, his or her conscience will protest. As I've already established, the protesting of the conscience is not to be confused with the accusation of the Enemy. The former is the *illumination* of the Spirit. Paul referred to it when he said, "Do not grieve the Holy Spirit" (Eph. 4:30).

Some people have alarm systems in their home. When the alarm system is turned on, the alarm will automatically go off if a person opens any door in the house. A similar thing happens when a believer opens a door to sin. The Holy Spirit through our awakened consciences protests. This is an automatic result of the spiritual alarm system that we were equipped with when we were born anew. Ignoring that alarm, or inward protest, is to suffer loss.

Is Repentance for Christians?

So what do you do when you open a forbidden door and the Holy Spirit protests in your conscience? The answer: repent. *Repentance* is a New Testament word. It applies not only to unbelievers but to believers when they engage in sinful conduct or attitudes (see 2 Corinthians 7, which is written to Christians).

Note Paul's words to the Corinthian believers:

> I am afraid that when I come again my God
> may humiliate me before you, and I may
> mourn over many of those who have sinned
> in the past and not repented of the impurity,
> immorality and sensuality which they have
> practiced. (2 Cor. 12:21)

Repentance means to have a change of mind. Some contemporary writers call it a mental U-turn. Unrepentant sin (sin that a believer hasn't changed his or her mind about) will produce turbulence in our spirits, and for good reason. In such cases, we shouldn't ignore our conscience just because Jesus shed His blood for our sins.

We shouldn't say, "That's guilt, so I'm going to ignore it. Jesus forgave all my sin." No, that inward feeling of unrest and regret will remain until we deal with it. By dealing with it, I mean changing our minds about whatever caused our consciences to protest, stopping the behavior, and making restitution to others when applicable. (If we stole something, then we return it. If we lied or slandered, we make it right. If we hurt someone, we issue an apology.)

If a person keeps suppressing his or her conscience when it's being pricked by the Holy Spirit and keeps ignoring the sense of spiritual unrest due to walking in a way that's contrary to the new nature in Christ, that person can "silence" his or her conscience, and its voice becomes deadened.

This isn't something that you or I want.

The fact is, there *are* spiritual consequences for walking in the flesh even though all of our sins have been forgiven. The Holy Spirit is a person, a real person, and He can be grieved by us as Paul said in Ephesians. He can also be quenched by our actions or attitudes (1 Thess. 5:19).

When a Christian grieves the Spirit, it registers in his or her conscience. This isn't "guilt" or "condemnation"—it's the enlightenment of the Spirit.

Regretting our sin is the fruit of God's work in our lives, and the Spirit will work such attitudes in our hearts if we let Him. Speaking to Christians in Judea, James exhorted those who sinned to humble themselves and sorrow over their transgressions (James 4:1–10). And that's in the New Testament.

The Power of the Blood

Hebrews exhorts us to come boldly to the "throne of grace" (4:16). Where God's people are concerned, Jesus Christ sits on a throne of grace, not a throne of judgment.

His throne is one of judgment to those who refuse to trust and follow Him. But if you have trusted Christ, His throne emits grace and mercy.

That said, if you are struggling with condemnation and guilt, I suggest you do two things:

1. Repent of all known sin. That means turning away from it. If you've sinned against someone directly, confess your sin to him or her.
2. Accept the fact that the blood of Jesus was enough to satisfy God, and it looms larger than your sin in His eyes. So receive the Lord's forgiveness by faith.

Consider this thought: When you feel condemned for something you've done wrong, you are essentially making yourself an idol. Why? Because you're setting your opinion over God's opinion.

There are many uncertainties in life. But there is one thing that is not uncertain: God's acceptance because of the blood of Jesus shed on your behalf. So arm your conscience with the reality of what the blood has done for you, and be set free from guilt and condemnation.

What the Blood of Christ Does

- It remits sins (Matt. 26:28 NKJV).
- It gives life to those who consume it (John 6:53).
- It causes us to dwell in Christ and Him in us (John 6:56).
- It is the means by which Jesus purchased the church (Acts 20:28).
- It is the means by which Jesus becomes our atonement through faith (Rom. 3:25).
- It justifies us and saves us from God's wrath (Rom. 5:9).
- It redeems us (Eph. 1:7; 1 Pet. 1:18–19; Rev. 5:9).
- It brings those who were far away from God near to Him (Eph. 2:13).

- It grants us the forgiveness of sins (Col. 1:14).
- It brings peace and reconciliation with God (Col. 1:20).
- It has "obtained eternal redemption" for us (Heb. 9:12).
- It cleanses our consciences from "dead works" to serve the living God (Heb. 9:14).
- It is the means by which we enter the Most Holy Place with boldness (Heb. 10:19 NIV).
- It "speaks a better word than the blood of Abel" (Heb. 12:24 NIV).
- It sanctifies us (Heb. 13:12).
- It makes us complete for "every good work" (Heb. 13:20–21 NKJV).
- It "cleanses us from all sin" (1 John 1:7).
- It bears witness in the earth along with the Spirit and the water (1 John 5:8 KJV).
- It is the means by which Jesus washes us (Rev. 1:5; 7:14 KJV).
- It is the means by which we overcome the accuser of the brethren (Rev. 12:10–11).

Thank God for the "precious blood" of Christ (1 Pet. 1:19), the "sprinkled blood" of Christ (Heb. 12:24), the blood of "the new covenant" (Luke 22:20), the "blood of the eternal covenant" shed for us (Heb. 13:20).

"The life ... is in the blood" (Lev. 17:11).

Our Advocate

As our great high priest, Jesus also acts as our advocate. This means that He is our defense attorney—or lawyer—who represents us and pleads our case. Sitting at the highest place in heaven, Christ is His people's defense attorney, not their prosecutor.

He is a representative of God, totally acceptable to the Father. As such, He makes the resources of heaven—including divine grace, power, and mercy—freely available to His people (Eph. 1:3).

> My little children, I am writing these things to you so that you may not sin. And if anyone sins, we have an Advocate with the Father, Jesus Christ the righteous; and He Himself is the propitiation for our sins; and not for ours only, but also for those of the whole world. (1 John 2:1–2)

Jesus isn't pleading your case before an angry God who wants to judge you for your sin. Instead, Christ stands alongside you as your advocate, removing the barriers that stand in the way of your fellowship with your Creator. He defends your case against "the accuser of our brethren," the Devil (Rev. 12:10).

Notice that John said, "We have an Advocate with the Father." This is a family matter.

Righteousness means right standing with God. It is the ability to stand in God's presence without shame. When you sin, your conscience lets you know. This is good and healthy. However, God's Enemy—who is called "the accuser of our brethren"—condemns you in your conscience "day and night" (Rev. 12:10). That's where the problem lies.

But thank God, there is One who moves on your behalf to defend you. What is more, He doesn't charge for His work, and He's never lost a case!

As our advocate, Jesus defends us—not on the basis of our own works or worthiness, but on the basis of His work on our behalf.

Because of the blood of Christ, we can come to God's throne boldly and with confidence. Jesus is a sympathetic high priest who understands our weaknesses, for He was tempted "in all points as we are" (Heb. 4:15 KJV).

In other words, the high-priestly ministry of Jesus Christ enables Him to identify with our struggles and temptations. We often think of Jesus as being unable to relate to us and our weaknesses because He was perfect and never sinned.

Yes, Jesus was perfect, and He never sinned. But He was subject to all the weaknesses and temptations to which we are subject. So much so that He personally relates to us in our struggles:

> Therefore, He had to be made like His brethren in all things, so that He might become a merciful and faithful high priest in things pertaining to God, to make propitiation for the sins of the people. For since He Himself was tempted in that which He has suffered, He is able to come to the aid of those who are tempted. (Heb. 2:17–18)

> For we do not have a high priest who cannot sympathize with our weaknesses, but One who has been tempted in all things as we are, yet without sin. Therefore let us draw near with confidence to the throne of grace, so that we may receive mercy and find grace to help in time of need. (Heb. 4:15–16)

In ourselves, we are not worthy to approach the holy presence of God. But we aren't in ourselves. *We are in Christ.*

Consequently, the high-priestly ministry of Jesus Christ gives us perpetual access to God the Father. Because of the cleansing of the blood (sprinkled on the mercy seat of God's throne) and "the washing of water with the word" (Eph. 5:26), we can come into God's holy presence with boldness.

> Therefore, brothers, since we have boldness to enter the sanctuary through the blood of Jesus, by a new and living way He has opened for us through the curtain (that is, His flesh), and since we have a great high priest over the house of God, let us draw near with a true heart in full assurance of faith, our hearts sprinkled clean from an evil conscience and our bodies washed in pure water. (Heb. 10:19–22 HCSB)

Paul echoed this thought, saying,

> He made Him who knew no sin to be sin on our behalf, so that we might become the righteousness of God in Him. (2 Cor. 5:21)

Our Intercessor

The high-priestly ministry of Jesus Christ also guarantees His constant intercession for us:

> Because [Jesus] continues forever, [He] holds
> His priesthood permanently. Therefore He is
> able also to save forever those who draw near
> to God through Him, since He always lives to
> make intercession for them. (Heb. 7:24–25)

> Who will bring a charge against God's elect? God
> is the one who justifies; who is the one who con-
> demns? Christ Jesus is He who died, yes, rather
> who was raised, who is at the right hand of God,
> who also intercedes for us. (Rom. 8:33–34)

While Jesus was on earth, He prayed for Peter (Luke
22:31–32). He also prayed for His disciples, including His
future disciples—which includes you and me (John 17).
However, I'm not sure Jesus is kneeling at the right hand of
God and praying for every single child of God on earth.

Rather, Jesus intercedes for us continually by virtue of the
wounds in His hands and feet, bearing our humanity before
the Father, persistently cleansing us of our sins and mediating
the new covenant to us (1 John 1:7–9):

> For there is one God, and one mediator also
> between God and men, the man Christ Jesus, who
> gave Himself as a ransom for all. (1 Tim. 2:5–6)

As our mediating high priest, Jesus saves sinners (1 Tim. 1:15); He "delivers us from the wrath to come" (1 Thess. 1:10 NKJV); He atones for our sins (Heb. 2:17); He is the guarantee and mediator of a new and better covenant (Heb. 7:22; 8:6; 9:15; 12:24); and He is our peace (Eph. 2:14). As the peace of God, Christ gives us unclouded access to God the Father, peace with ourselves, and peace in our consciences.

> Consequently, he is able to save to the uttermost those who draw near to God through him, since he always lives to make intercession for them. (Heb. 7:25 ESV)

If we have an uttermost need, Jesus is the uttermost Savior to meet it. His ministry at the right hand of God is tireless and unceasing. He ever lives to make intercession for us.

Since the sixteenth century, Christians have called John 17 the Lord's High Priestly Prayer. Because Jesus is the sinless, perfect Son of God, His prayers—which include the prayer in John 17—are always answered. That's good news for every child of God.

Sitting, Standing, and Walking

The New Testament repeatedly says that since His ascension, Jesus has been sitting at the right hand of God the Father in heavenly realms (Acts 2:33; 5:31; Rom. 8:34; Heb. 1:3; 8:1; 10:12; 1 Pet. 3:22).

The "right hand" is a metaphor that speaks of the authority, power, and universal rule emanating from God's throne.

Yet when Stephen was being stoned, he peered into the heavens and saw Jesus standing—not sitting—at God's right hand (Acts 7:55–56). This, to me, indicates that Jesus was cheering for Stephen, awaiting his arrival in heavenly places.

From the book of Revelation, we learn that Jesus also "walks" in the midst of His churches, typified by golden lampstands (Rev. 2:1). So Christ sits, Christ stands, and Christ walks in His present-day ministry.

Interestingly, Paul told us in the book of Ephesians that the Christian *sits* in heavenly places with Christ (1:20; 2:6), *walks* in the world (4:1, 17), and stands against the Enemy (6:11, 13). Thus we mirror the same three postures our Lord uses.

Because Jesus is our great high priest, we have a friend in high places. We have connections with the Creator. So we can always come to the throne of grace and pour out our hearts to the Lord, and we will not be turned away.

Jesus Christ is a perfect high priest, a perfect advocate, a perfect intercessor, and a perfect mediator who has given us a perfect covenant with God.

As such, He saves us from the wrath to come. He saves us from guilt and condemnation. He saves us from ourselves.

As we saw in Hebrews 7:25, Jesus "saves us to the uttermost" (ESV).

He is also a "high priest after the order of Melchizedek" (Heb. 5:10 ESV), which means His priesthood is eternal, universal, and perfect (Ps. 110:4; Heb. 5:6–10; 6:20; 7:1–26).

Like Melchizedek, Jesus is both priest and king. He is a mediator who is both God and man, one person in two natures.

Hebrews 13:20 speaks of the "eternal covenant." Jesus has no successor as high priest because His once-and-for-all sacrifice obtained eternal redemption for us. In other words, the eternal Son gives us eternal salvation in which we can be secure forever. There's nothing that can be added to it.

Remember: There's a throne of grace waiting for you. Consequently, don't run away from Jesus when you sin. Run to Him.

The Christ we live with daily is a practical high priest! He has invested in us, moment by moment. It's not about a ritual or some sort of useless head knowledge that doesn't affect our everyday lives. It's about reality and experience. Because Jesus is your high priest, you cannot lose. Get ahold of these realities and believe them. They will change your life.

CHAPTER 2

CHIEF SHEPHERD

When the Chief Shepherd appears, you will
receive the unfading crown of glory.

1 Peter 5:4

A friend of mine tells his story of traveling through the steppes of Afghanistan and the northern regions of Iran and being struck by the pastoral style of life present there.

It's a simple life, relatively the same as it was two thousand years ago when peasants moved from site to site, herding their livestock. One day my friend, through a translator, asked an older herdsman what the greatest challenge of being a shepherd was. His response, given in a measured chuckle, was: "Getting the sheep to know that

I'm the shepherd, and they're not!" This about sums up the Christian life, doesn't it?

While He was on earth, Jesus described Himself as the *good* shepherd, and one of His foremost disciples called Him "the Chief Shepherd" (1 Pet. 5:4):

> I am the good shepherd; the good shepherd lays down His life for the sheep. He who is a hired hand, and not a shepherd, who is not the owner of the sheep, sees the wolf coming, and leaves the sheep and flees, and the wolf snatches them and scatters them. He flees because he is a hired hand and is not concerned about the sheep. I am the good shepherd, and I know My own and My own know Me, even as the Father knows Me and I know the Father; and I lay down My life for the sheep. (John 10:11–15)

Since His resurrection, He is also called "the great Shepherd of the sheep":

> Now the God of peace, who brought up from the dead the great Shepherd of the sheep through the blood of the eternal covenant, even Jesus our Lord. (Heb. 13:20)

What exactly is the Lord's role as chief shepherd? And what does it mean when He calls Himself "the *good* shepherd"? These are questions I've wondered about for quite some time. Perhaps the best text in the entire Bible that answers them is Psalm 23. Let's look at it with an eye to understanding the present-day ministry of Jesus Christ.

On Shepherds and Sheep

Sheep are the most frequently mentioned animal in all of Scripture, and God's people are often depicted in the Bible as sheep.

David, who wrote Psalm 23, was a shepherd by trade. He had an intimate knowledge of shepherding and sheep. I've always thought that was interesting. David was perhaps the greatest king in all of Israelite history, and certainly the founder of an entire dynasty of rulers.

Usually when a king or a ruler in ancient cultures came to power, he rewrote his backstory. Think of Octavian, the nephew of Julius Caesar, rising to power. What did he do? He changed his name to Augustus (which means "one worthy of worship") and had several new biographies commissioned, each one linking him to the gods and heroes of Roman mythology.

But with David we see something different. It seems that when people remembered him, they proudly recalled

his humble beginnings. I wonder why. I believe that being
a shepherd—being attached to sheep—was not only a valid
way of living but was also recognized as a way of being deeply
connected with God's own heart.

Shepherding is fit for a king because it reflects the occupation of the Creator of all things. Many of David's songs point
to Christ. This is no more true than with several of his shepherd's songs. Interestingly, Psalm 22, 23, and 24 all foreshadow
different aspects of Christ's ministry.

Psalm 22 points to Christ's crucifixion (past).

Psalm 24 points to His second coming (future).

And right in the middle, Psalm 23 points to the Lord's
present-day ministry. Thus it is a text that firmly belongs
to us.

> The LORD is my shepherd,
> I shall not want.
> He makes me lie down in green pastures;
> He leads me beside quiet waters.
> He restores my soul;
> He guides me in the paths of righteousness
> For His name's sake.
>
> Even though I walk through the valley of the
>   shadow of death,

I fear no evil, for You are with me;

Your rod and Your staff, they comfort me.

You prepare a table before me in the presence

of my enemies;

You have anointed my head with oil;

My cup overflows.

Surely goodness and lovingkindness will

follow me all the days of my life,

And I will dwell in the house of the LORD

forever.

Let's break down each part of this passage with an eye toward understanding the present-day ministry of Christ as our great shepherd.

Ownership

The LORD is my shepherd ...

The quality of a sheep's life depends mostly on the kind of shepherd who takes care of it. If the shepherd is selfish and neglectful, the sheep will suffer. If the shepherd is watchful and caring, the sheep will thrive.

We have the greatest shepherd in the universe: Jesus Christ. He gave His own precious life for you, His sheep. You can't get more unselfish and caring than that. And He continues to care for you as a shepherd.

In fact, God created sheep and shepherds to show us the relationship we have with Jesus. Think about it. It's all an image and a shadow of something more real.

Sheep require human care to survive. They are the most needy and dependent of all animals. They are incapable of caring for themselves. God created them to require enormous attention.

In the Middle Ages, one of the most common metaphors for the "divine right to rule" described the king as a shepherd and the peasants as sheep. It was said that ordinary people needed the "blue bloods" to guide and direct them. It wasn't until Jacques Rousseau and the French Revolution that this logic was challenged. Rousseau's argument went something like this: we are *all* sheep, and our *Lord* isn't someone else—it's actually Christ Himself.

Unlike many of the cruel and exacting rulers of the world, Jesus is a shepherd who enjoys caring for you. So much so that He calls you His own.

Old Testament shepherds would mark the ears of their sheep to show who owned them. In the same way, Jesus has put His mark on you. He's "marked you" from the foundation of the world and called you His own (Eph. 1:4–5).

Having bought you with the price of His own blood, Jesus is the rightful "Guardian" of your soul:

> For you were continually straying like sheep,
> but now you have returned to the Shepherd
> and Guardian of your souls. (1 Pet. 2:25)

Supply

I shall not want ...

This statement indicates that the Lord's sheep do not lack anything. There are no deficiencies.

How does this work out in real life, you might ask? This statement asks us to believe that whatever we need is in the care of our shepherd, and He will supply it. It may not come in the form we expect or wish, but He will eventually meet the need.

There's an interesting story in which a woman dreamed that she went to heaven. To her astonishment, paradise was depicted as a grocery store. When she went to the cash register, she discovered that God Himself was sitting behind the counter.

God pleasantly asked her what her heart's desire was. She didn't really know, so she began to dream out loud. She wished for a better life for herself, for her friends, and for the friends of her friends. She asked for the solution to world suffering and for an end to all wars.

The woman continued to wish for orphanages, halfway houses, and schools ... until she noticed God smirking.

Stopping, she asked what was so funny. His reply was simple: "Oh, my child—I'm sorry; this really isn't that kind of store. We're not a produce stand. We're a seed shop!"

God isn't in the business of supplying our wishes and dreams. Rather, He equips us with the seeds to abundance, supplying our needs as He knows, which is often different from what we might imagine.

The truth is, the good shepherd casts a watchful eye over His sheep to make sure they are loved and cared for. Even when they are asleep, He watches over them. He wants His sheep to come to Him if they have a deficiency, trusting that He will meet it.

Total dependence and trust are what He is after. The biblical word for these things is *faith*.

Rest

He makes me lie down in green pastures …

Sheep will not lie down if they are afraid. Neither can they find rest if they are bothered by other sheep or insects or are hungry. Sheep must be completely at peace before they can sleep.

It is the shepherd's job to ensure that a sheep is content enough to relax. Sheep are easily startled. This makes them among the most timid animals on the planet.

The main thing that causes a sheep to feel safe and secure

is to spot the shepherd. Seeing the shepherd relieves the sheep's anxiety and puts it at ease. It also causes a sheep to be at peace with other sheep.

In the same way, being conscious of the presence of Jesus relieves our fears and causes us to rest. The presence of Christ causes us to forget about our squabbles with others, which are often rooted in selfish ambition and pride.

It is the present-day ministry of Jesus, through the Holy Spirit, that gives us calm in the midst of life's storms. It is His presence that relieves us from parasites and other pests that disturb our peace. And it is His nearness that causes us to lose all sense of rivalry and competition with others.

The shepherd's job is to clear the ground of roots, stumps, and weeds and to ensure that there is fresh grass for the sheep to find rest. Again, hungry sheep can only stand.

Jesus, our good shepherd, provides us with spiritual food so that we can rest contented. This is available to all of God's children, if we only avail ourselves of it.

Refreshment

He leads me beside quiet waters …

Typically, sheep rise before dawn and begin to eat. If there is heavy dew on the grass, sheep can go for months without actually drinking. One of the jobs of the shepherd, then, is to provide water for the sheep.

In the Gospels, Jesus had a lot to say about thirst and drinking.

Go to the well that never runs dry. You don't ever need to thirst again. On the other hand, substitutes like drugs, fame, possessions, and sex will all eventually run dry.

Jesus gives us water to drink. Just like the real food we are given to eat, the real water is Himself.

> "If you knew the gift of God, and who it is who says to you, 'Give Me a drink,' you would have asked Him, and He would have given you living water." ... Jesus answered and said to [the Samaritan woman], "Everyone who drinks of this water will thirst again; but whoever drinks of the water that I will give him shall never thirst; but the water that I will give him will become in him a well of water springing up to eternal life." (John 4:10, 13–14)

> As the living Father hath sent me, and I live by the Father: so he that eateth me, even he shall live by me. (John 6:57 KJV)

Encouragement

He restores my soul ...

Like humans, sheep can feel cast down, discouraged, and dejected. A sheep that is "cast down" on its back will eventually die if someone doesn't put it back on its feet. It is the shepherd's job to keep count of the sheep in the flock, for if one is missing, it could very well be cast down somewhere.

If it's a hot day, a downcast sheep could die within hours if it isn't put back on its feet.

When the Lord's true sheep are cast down, either because of falling, failure, or frustration, the Lord doesn't abandon ship and leave them to die. No. He instead comes alongside them to put them back on their feet. He is the restorer of their souls.

A sheep that has too much wool can easily fall. In the Bible, wool speaks of self-effort. For this reason, the priests in the Old Testament couldn't wear wool. Meaning, they couldn't sweat. They instead wore linen, which prevented them from sweating.

Trying to serve the Lord in our own strength and power eventually leads to being cast down. Either we stumble and fall, or we become frustrated and burned out.

Fat sheep also are in danger of falling over. Consequently,

the self-indulgent Christian who doesn't deny himself or herself is in danger of being cast down.

In either case, Jesus, our great shepherd, is present to pick us back up and put us on our feet. We simply have to be willing to let Him do His work of restoration.

Guidance

> *He guides me in the paths of righteousness*
> *for His name's sake ...*

Sheep are habitual creatures. They will do the same thing the same way regardless of the consequences. For example, they'll graze from the same plot of grass until the ground is desolate. Consequently, the shepherd must keep his sheep moving. This includes guiding them to different pastures from time to time.

Sheep are not just stupid; they are stubborn. Isaiah 53:6 captures this characteristic:

> All of us like sheep have gone astray,
> Each of us has turned to his own way.

Jesus, our good shepherd, leads us into His paths lest we ruin ourselves and others. He will lead us into new territory if we will submit ourselves to His guidance, preferring it over our own independent ideas.

In addition, a good shepherd will never take his sheep where he hasn't gone himself. So, too, when the Lord Jesus Christ leads us by His Spirit, He essentially causes us to relive His own life. That would include dying to self (crucified with Him), living by His life (raised with Him), and gaining our victory over the forces of darkness (seated with Him in heavenly places).

Christ is our forerunner and trailblazer, always going ahead of us:

> Jesus has entered as a forerunner for us, having become a high priest forever according to the order of Melchizedek. (Heb. 6:20)

Assurance

> *Even though I walk through the valley of the shadow of death, I fear no evil, for You are with me …*

In every grueling trial, in every dark night, in every unexpected crisis, our good shepherd promises to be with us. Therefore, we have nothing to fear.

All throughout the Bible, God tells His people to "fear not." As sheep, we are naturally fearful, untrusting, and timid.

But Jesus is greater than any problem. He has all authority in heaven and on earth. There is nothing that He cannot handle.

However, He wishes to take us to the high mountains. But this requires that we pass through and climb the valleys. Not only will He lead us through the valleys, but He will also walk with us there.

> Fear not, little flock; for it is your Father's good
> pleasure to give you the kingdom. (Luke 12:32
> KJV)

Consequently, most of the dilemmas, distresses, and disappointments we experience are crafted by the hand of God to bring us to higher ground.

Even in the dark valleys, God feeds His sheep. Interestingly, the valleys provide the richest feed and the best forage for the sheep. There is also water there. So the Lord meets us in the valley with food and drink. We are often unaware of this until we get past the crisis and look back to see God's hand of care and protection.

Having been through dark valleys ourselves, we may offer the Lord's comfort to those who are walking in dark valleys now:

> Blessed be the God and Father of our Lord
> Jesus Christ, the Father of mercies and God of

all comfort, who comforts us in all our affliction so that we will be able to comfort those
who are in any affliction with the comfort with
which we ourselves are comforted by God.
(2 Cor. 1:3–4)

Correction

Your rod and Your staff, they comfort me ...

The rod and the staff are the shepherd's arsenal. The rod is used
to defend the shepherd and his sheep from predators. It's also
used to discipline wayward sheep and bring them back to the
flock.

The shepherd's staff is his hallmark instrument. The staff is
a long, slender stick with a hook at the end of it. The shepherd
uses his staff to bring newborn lambs to their mothers. He also
uses it to draw sheep closer to one another or to himself (for
examination). Unlike the rod, the staff is used gently.

Both instruments express the care and concern that the
shepherd has for his sheep. For this reason, the shepherd's rod
and staff bring comfort to the sheep.

In the same way, the Lord Jesus Christ defends, disciplines,
and draws us closer to Himself and to the other members of
His body via His "rod" and His "staff."

Protection

You prepare a table before me in the presence of my enemies ...

Before spring, a shepherd of Israel would make a trip to survey the wild country, looking for a new "tableland" to keep his flock. Before the sheep arrived at the new territory, the shepherd would roll up his sleeves and do the hard work of pulling up poisonous plants, clearing the debris, and opening up the springs and waterholes.

This was all preparatory work.

Jesus Christ, our chief shepherd, goes before us to prepare the way for every encounter we will face.

Sometimes He will deliver us *from* troubles that lie ahead. But other times He will carry us *through* those troubles. Rather than remove them, He will bless us in the midst of the storm. This is just as miraculous as His deliverance.

Paul's thorn in the flesh is an example. The Lord chose not to remove the thorn; He rather chose to cause Paul to endure.

So sometimes our good shepherd will ward off our enemies with the rod of His judgment, while other times He will prepare a feast for us in the presence of our enemies.

Healing

You have anointed my head with oil; my cup overflows ...

During the summer months, sheep are often brutalized by pests. These include mosquitoes, gnats, and nose flies. All are profoundly irritating to the sheep, often causing extreme inflammation.

To get relief, the sheep will sometimes beat its head against trees, rocks, or other objects. Sometimes the tormenting pests will cause the sheep to stop eating. In more severe cases, the infection from the pests can cause a sheep to go blind.

The antidote is for the shepherd to anoint the sheep's head with oil. The oil wards off the sheep's tormentors and aids in healing its wounds. As a result, the sheep can eat again. The oil, however, must be applied regularly for it to have a sustaining effect.

All throughout the Bible, oil is a symbol of the Holy Spirit. Jesus, our good shepherd, ministers His Spirit to us, and the Spirit brings healing, freedom, and peace. However, a fresh supply of the Spirit must repeatedly be given. So Paul exhorted his readers to be continually "filled with the Spirit" (Eph. 5:18).

Blessing

Surely goodness and lovingkindness will
follow me all the days of my life ...

This is a great promise. Almost too good to be true. Romans 8:28 contains echoes of it:

And we know that all things work together for
good to them that love God, to them who are
the called according to his purpose. (KJV)

No matter what is thrown at you in this life, "surely"—
which means "of a certainty"—goodness and lovingkindness
will follow you all the days of your life.

Your shepherd's love will never leave you. And He will
see to it that all things in your life—whether pleasant or
unpleasant—will work for your good.

When the smoke cleared after one particularly dark
period in my life, I came out on the other side with a sense
that God's goodness and love had not only followed me but
hounded me. It was as though I couldn't escape even if I had
wanted to. Like Jonah attempting to sneak away from God's
will, only to find himself accompanied by the Almighty in
the belly of a whale, we often discover that our bleakest
hour is filled with God's companionship. His goodness and
mercy hunt and chase us down.

A wonderful promise indeed, especially during the dark
seasons of our lives. Our good shepherd will eventually bring
beauty and blessing out of the chaos.

Interestingly, if sheep are mishandled and poorly managed,
as we mentioned earlier, they can destroy a piece of land in no
time. On the other hand, if they are managed properly by a

good and wise shepherd, they can be some of the most benefi-
cial animals for the land. They can clean up and repair a piece
of wrecked turf in a short period of time.

It all depends on the kind of shepherd who is managing
the sheep.

So, too, those who follow the chief shepherd don't have goodness and lovingkindness simply coming to them. Rather, goodness
and lovingkindness *follow them* wherever they go, benefiting and
blessing others.

Security

And I will dwell in the house of the LORD forever ...

This is where the Twenty-third Psalm transforms from a
simple meditation on sheep into a direct commentary on
the daily love life between believers and their Lord. It is
the shepherd's presence that makes all of the things previ-
ously listed (green pastures, refreshing waters, anointing oil,
etc.) a possibility. That presence isn't found everywhere. It's
located in one very specific place: His house. In the New
Testament we discover that we, collectively as believers, are
God's house. By holding on to Christ, we are transformed
from individuals into the unified household of God. In this
psalm we read a similar reality—that by being in relationship

with the chief shepherd, we are brought into connection with His house.

The psalm ends by promising that the presence of the great shepherd will always be with His sheep. The Lord's sheep will remain in His house forever.

Over the years, many people have expressed to me their skepticism about the experience of Christian community that I have often described in my earlier books.[1] I have a friend who calls my view and practice of church "dormitory-style Christianity." This is pretty close to the mark. But keep in mind, if it's uncomfortable to imagine being in close relationship with believers today, some of us may be disappointed in eternity—as we will dwell in God's house, His body, forever. There is an eternal connectedness among those who follow the Lord that extends endlessly in every direction.

This is not only a promise of being part of God's flock—the *ekklesia*, His house. It's also a promise that His presence will never leave us, in this life or in the life after.

When hard times come our way, the Lord may sometimes appear to have quit His job. But although He may not seem present, our good shepherd is never absent. The guardian of our souls never sleeps. He never forgets to watch over us. He

---

1   See *Reimagining Church* (David C Cook, 2008) and *From Eternity to Here* (David C Cook, 2009) for details.

never leaves us or forsakes us. His ear is always attuned to our cries.

In John 10, Jesus made it clear that because we are His sheep, we know His voice. Jesus is not our shepherd because we believe. We believe because He is our shepherd and we are His sheep.

Insofar as we follow the voice of the chief shepherd, we will remain safe, secure, and pleasing to His heart.

CHAPTER 3

HEAVENLY BRIDEGROOM

Christ also loved the church and gave Himself up for her, so that He might sanctify her, having cleansed her by the washing of water with the word, that He might present to Himself the church in all her glory, having no spot or wrinkle or any such thing; but that she would be holy and blameless.

Ephesians 5:25–27

Recently I came across a story about a young couple in the middle of a crisis. One afternoon, surrounded by dirty dishes, a pile of diapers from their two-year-old daughter, and a laundry list of household chores still to be done, the young wife stood sobbing.

She'd had enough. Through streaming tears she gathered her bags and left. She didn't exactly know where she was going, and she didn't have to. She simply knew that she could not keep playing the role of wife and mother any longer.

The husband was devastated. Left alone with a little daughter and mounting bills, he was frazzled and angry. His first evening alone, the phone rang—it was his wife! He snatched up the receiver and demanded to know where she was and what was going on. He then told her she must come home. She immediately hung up. The husband cursed and clanked the phone back down. This little ritual went on night after night. She would call, and he would angrily and aggressively respond.

But as the days turned into weeks, he gradually began to shift his attitude. What could he do, after all? That's when he decided something. The young husband hired a private investigator and discovered where his wife was staying. She was residing in another town several hours away. The husband drove the distance and found himself standing in front of the hotel door, knocking. His wife answered. The look of shock on her face melted into one of grateful sobs. She then collapsed into his arms.

Sometime later he asked her why, exactly, she came back with him that evening, when before there had been so many missed opportunities, crossed wires, and unmet requests to come home.

Her response was simple: "Before, when you asked me to come home, it was only words. But finally, you came to where I was. That made all the difference."

Besides being our high priest and chief shepherd, Jesus Christ is our lover. In fact, He's the greatest lover in the universe—not in a cheap or sentimental way, but because He comes to where we are. The final verses of the book of Ephesians resound with this theme: "Husbands, love your wives, just as Christ also loved the church and gave Himself up for her" (Eph. 5:25)! What a bridegroom!

God put romance into His creation. He put romance into the heart of man and woman. He put romance into His holy Word.

He invented the idea.

In fact, all true romances are a pale image of the sacred romance that runs like a golden thread from Genesis to Revelation.

In Part One of *From Eternity to Here*, I traced this golden thread, showing that God's eternal purpose is to obtain a bride for His Son.

In Genesis we see Adam, the first man ever created. Adam is alone, and God puts him in a deep sleep. While he is sleeping, God reaches into Adam's side and pulls out a woman. The woman is called Eve.

Adam awakens, and upon looking at Eve, he falls in love. At last he has found a companion, and he is no longer alone. The two then become one.

So when Adam walked around the earth, he had a girl inside of him until God took her out. God split the Adam, as it were, and then the two became one again.

In Ephesians 5, Paul spoke about this and made a shocking statement:

> No one ever hated his own flesh, but nourishes and cherishes it, just as Christ also does the church, because we are members of His body. For this reason a man shall leave his father and mother and shall be joined to his wife, and the two shall become one flesh. This mystery is great; but I am speaking with reference to Christ and the church. (vv. 29–32)

Jesus Christ was put into a deep sleep by His Father on Calvary. And when Jesus died, His side was pierced, and out of it flowed water and blood.

All throughout the Bible, the blood speaks of redemption and the water speaks of cleansing and life.

While Jesus was in a deep sleep, God brought forth the new Eve, the church of the living God, from Christ's side. And she was in Christ "before the foundation of the world" (Eph. 1:4).

When Jesus walked around the earth, He had a girl inside of Him—the most beautiful girl in the world. And when He died and rose from the dead, she was born. Christ's pierced side was the womb from which she came. And the two—Christ and the church—are one.

> The one who joins himself to the Lord is one
> spirit with Him. (1 Cor. 6:17)

God's Ultimate Passion

From before creation, God the Father ordained that He would give His Son an eternal companion who would meet His beating heart.

He would cherish her, and she would love Him back. And she, the bride, would reign with Him on His throne.

The Lord doesn't force her to be His. Instead, He woos her to Himself and cherishes her. This is what He is doing now as our bridegroom.

First, He woos us and overtakes us with His love. Then He begins His work of making us ready for that great wedding day when the bride will become the wife of the Lamb, perfected into His likeness:

> For I am jealous for you with a godly jealousy; for
> I betrothed you to one husband, so that to Christ
> I might present you as a pure virgin. (2 Cor. 11:2)

For the marriage of the Lamb has come and His bride has made herself ready. (Rev. 19:7)

Then one of the seven angels who had the seven bowls full of the seven last plagues came and spoke with me, saying, "Come here, I will show you the bride, the wife of the Lamb." (Rev. 21:9)

Jesus Is Seeking Lovers

Just as Adam desired a companion, a helpmeet, and a lover, Jesus is seeking lovers—those who will return His love.

Unfortunately, many believers today have made the Christian life only about serving. They teach that Christians are servants, those who obey the Master.

While it is true that we are servants for the Lord, this idea alone misses an important dimension. Jesus is looking for lovers, not maids. He's looking for intimate companions, not forced slaves.

The Lord is looking for something way beyond mandatory obedience. He desires voluntary lovers. Those who have been captured by His love. Those who have been captivated by the sight of His stunning worth. Those who have allowed His love to penetrate their beings and return it to Him.

Any love that we have for Jesus is a reflection of His love for us.

> We love him, because he first loved us. (1 John
> 4:19 KJV)

Whether you are a male or a female, you are part of a girl—the most beautiful woman in the world. And your Lord is madly in love with her.

Astoundingly, the Lord said that He loves His bride with the same intense love with which the Father loves Him:

> Just as the Father has loved Me, I have also
> loved you; abide in My love. (John 15:9)

> That the love with which You [the Father] loved
> Me may be in them. (John 17:26)

Consequently, Jesus cannot love us any more than He loves us now. He proved this at Calvary.

Songs for the Bride

As I've pointed out elsewhere, the Bible begins with a marriage, and it ends with a marriage. It begins with a boy and a girl, and it ends with a boy and a girl. Jesus began His ministry by stating that He was the bridegroom (Matt. 9:15), and He ended His ministry by talking about the bride (Matt. 25:1–13).

John the Baptist introduced Jesus to the world. And when he did, he called Jesus the bridegroom (John 3:29). And at the end of the story, the bridegroom and the bride will become one (Rev. 22:17). This has been God's plan from the beginning.

What follows are two songs written by organic missional churches that express the Lord's love for His bride and the bride's love for Him.

I believe these two songs will help bring home the unbridled passion that beats in the heart of Your Lord for His counterpart.

SONG FOR THE BRIDE 1[1]

(Sung to the tune of "Hallelujah" by Leonard Cohen and Theresa Christina Calonge de Sa Mattos)

---

1   Go to frankviola.org/creativity to watch a video of a live performance of this song.

Sisters:

I heard there was a secret chord,
that David played and it pleased You, Lord.
The mystery of the ages hidden in You.

It goes like this: the birth, the gift,
the minor fall, the major lift.
The risen King commanding hallelujah.

CHORUS

Hallelujah, hallelujah, hallelujah, hallelujah.

Brothers:

I knew you were creation's song.
In the garden we walked along.
My presence and My kinship offered to you.

But you took a bite from a different tree.
Another life that's not from Me,
and from your lips it stripped My hallelujah.

SILENT CHORUS

Sisters:

Jesus, I've been here before.
I know this room and I've walked this floor.
I used to live alone before I knew You.

Now I've seen your death on the wooden arch.
Love is not a victory march.
It's a cold and it's a broken hallelujah.

CHORUS

Hallelujah, hallelujah, hallelujah, hallelujah.

Brothers:

I came to earth, I gave My life,
for you to be My eternal wife.
I tell the truth, I died to never lose you.

And now I live and move in you,
the Holy Dove is moving through,
and every breath you draw is hallelujah.

CHORUS

All:

And now we live so all can know
what's really going on below.
Your sacrifice restoring all things to You.

Together with a heavenly throng
we'll stand before the Lord of song
with nothing on our tongue but hallelujah.

SONG FOR THE BRIDE 2

(Sung to the tune of "Over the Rainbow")

Brothers:

My bride, you have been chosen before time
Blessed with all of your glory
Blameless before My sight

Sisters:

My Lord, You're all I long for, I need You
All the dreams that I dare to dream
Really are of You

Brothers:

Each day I take you in My arms

Sisters:

And dance with me beyond the stars

All:

Together

Brothers:

I live in you and you in Me

Sisters:

Entwined for all eternity

All:

How You complete me

All:

My Love, I want to give you everything
True love, joy, and devotion
All that you are to me
Beholding you I always find
How truly you are
Kind of my own kind!

The Bridegroom's Desire

As the bride of Christ, the church is called to commune with, love, enthrone, and intimately know the heavenly bridegroom who indwells her.

Churches that excel in the bridal dimension give time and attention to spiritual fellowship with the Lord. Worship is a priority.

Seeking the Lord, loving Him, communing with Him, and just spending time with Him are central to His heart.

This dimension of the church can be seen as the engine that drives all of the church's activities. It is love from Christ and for Christ that is the church's motivation, energy, and life.

The Lord Jesus, as our heavenly bridegroom, doesn't see His church as a workforce. He wants lovers, not just helpers. Companions, not just servants.

The bridal dimension of the church is central to the church's life and mission.

Preparing the Bride

God the Father has been orchestrating history to prepare Christ's bride for marriage and reigning.

Each generation is working for the next. Every time a group of Christians and individual believers touch the heart of God and stand for His eternal purpose in the earth, a little bit of gold, pearl, and precious stone is deposited in the New Jerusalem for the building of God's eternal home.

One day, the bride will be prepared, and she will become the Lord's wife.

A compelling case can be made that God's greatest desire is to be known and loved. And He has woven this same desire in the heart of every human. Herein do we find the longing of Jesus as our heavenly bridegroom and our high calling as His bride.

How Important Is She?

The bride of Christ appears all throughout the Scriptures, from Genesis (in type and shadow) to Revelation. For example:

She (the church) appears in the opening pages of holy

Scripture, and she reappears at the very end (Eve in Genesis 2 and the bride in Revelation 22).

Your Lord and my Lord is consumed with a zeal that eats Him up for her. Jesus Christ gave His life for her and forsook everything to have her. (Ephesians 5:25 says that Christ gave Himself for the church. She's the "pearl of great price," hidden in God from before the ages.)

Jesus Christ sees Himself as indistinguishable from the church. She is bone of His bone and flesh of His flesh, His very body on earth (Matt. 25:40, 45; Acts 9:1–5).

She's the fiancée of the Son of God, and He's waiting to marry her.

Paul said in effect, "You, the body of Christ in Corinth, are the corporate Christ" (1 Cor. 12:12, 27; see also 1:12–13; 6:15; 8:12).

Some of the last words of Scripture are uttered by the bride: "The Spirit and the bride say, 'Come!'" (Rev. 22:17).

She's the wife of the Lamb. His partner for eternity.

She is at the very center of the mystery of the ages that Paul unveiled in Colossians and Ephesians.

The *ekklesia* is God's eternal purpose. From before creation, He has wanted a bride, a house, a family, and a body (a visible expression). That was His original intention.

From the beginning, God the Father has wanted a corporate expression of Himself to reveal the beauty of His Son. He desired to have a counterpart for His Son. Why was Eve made? For Adam, to be his counterpart.

Thus the church is not only important but is the most important thing to God that exists.

She's His girl.

When a man falls in love with a woman, there is nothing more important to him than her. That's a picture of the passion your Lord has for you.

Therefore, a large part of Christ's ministry today is to love, cherish, protect, and perfect His bride. And He desires that she return that love to Him.

CHAPTER 4

AUTHOR AND FINISHER OF OUR FAITH

Looking unto Jesus the author and finisher of our faith.

Hebrews 12:2 KJV

Beyond being our high priest, chief shepherd, and heavenly bridegroom, Jesus Christ is able to complete what He began in us.

This aspect of His present-day ministry has to do with spiritual growth and transformation. Not only is Christ in heavenly places interceding for us; He's also within every believer by His Spirit, forming His character within each of His disciples.

One of the most incredible promises in all of the Bible is Paul's statement in Philippians 1:6:

> I am confident of this very thing, that He who
> began a good work in you will perfect it until
> the day of Christ Jesus.

Paul was confident: what Jesus Christ began in your life will be completed.

Consequently, when you feel discouraged that you're not growing like you want to ... when you feel depressed that you keep having the same struggles and challenges ... when you don't see any progress in your spiritual life, remember: He who brought you to Himself *will* eventually perfect you. He *will* complete the work that He began in you, for He is the author and finisher of our faith.

Jesus said that He is "the way, the truth, and the life" (John 14:6 HCSB). Consider the word *life*. Just what is "life"—the beginning, the middle, or the end of it?

Is life more about the birth, the growth, or the maturing? We need to decide. I say this with a wink and a smile. We would never say that life is any of those things. Life is all of them and every point in between. Life is up and down, backward and forward, breathing and holding our breath. Life is about stopping and starting, action and reaction, giving and taking.

Life is! And the same can be said of Jesus Christ. He is the Alpha and the Omega. He is the beginning and the end. The

A to Z. He is the one at the starting point and at the end, at the same moment. And His life is deposited within all believers when they repent and believe upon Him. But that's not the end. That life—His life—grows in us and shapes our characters (Gal. 4:19). If we allow it to.

Our Regenerator

According to the Bible, human birth, growth, and development are images of our spiritual development.

First, Jesus saves us. This includes our justification on the one hand and our regeneration on the other. Regeneration is new birth, and birth is the impartation of life.

When Jesus rose from the dead, He became "a life-giving spirit" (1 Cor. 15:45). As such, He was able to "breathe" His Spirit into the disciples (John 20:22).

Jesus still does this for all who trust in Him today. When He breathes His Spirit into us, the seed of God's own life enters our dead spirits. We are raised to life and born anew:

> Jesus answered [Nicodemus], "Truly, truly, I say to you, unless one is born again he cannot see the kingdom of God." (John 3:3 ESV)

Therefore, if anyone is in Christ, he is a new
creation. The old has passed away; behold, the
new has come. (2 Cor. 5:17 ESV)

You have been born again, not of perishable
seed but of imperishable, through the living
and abiding word of God. (1 Pet. 1:23 ESV; see
also 1 Pet. 1:3–5; 2 Pet. 1:4; Titus 3:5; James
1:18; 1 John 3:9)

Spiritual Growth

The Bible speaks of three main stages in spiritual development
that correspond to our physical development: infancy, childhood, and adulthood.

The first stage is infancy:

Put away all malice and all deceit and hypocrisy
and envy and all slander. Like newborn infants,
long for the pure spiritual milk, that by it you
may grow up into salvation—if indeed you have
tasted that the Lord is good. (1 Pet. 2:1–3 ESV)

I, brothers, could not address you as spiritual
people, but as people of the flesh, as infants in

Christ. I fed you with milk, not solid food, for you
were not ready for it. And even now you are not
yet ready, for you are still of the flesh. For while
there is jealousy and strife among you, are you not
of the flesh and behaving only in a human way?
(1 Cor. 3:1–3 ESV)

Infancy is characterized by a kind of helplessness. A baby is
totally dependent on her or his parents to provide. This is true
both for the infant's external and internal needs. Just as a baby
needs milk, a baby also needs endless amounts of compassion and
love.

I can remember a friend suggesting that crying babies should
be disciplined. How ridiculous! Infants are simply alerting us to
their needs when they cry. There's a special sensitivity that we give
to infants in part because they are so helpless. But as they grow, we
increase the level of responsibility we give them.

The second stage of spiritual growth is childhood. Jesus sanctifies us by His Spirit, making us progressively holy in our conduct.
So we are first babes in Christ, and then we grow into childhood—
or as John put it, the stage of being "young [people]" in the faith:

I am writing to you, little children,
    because your sins are forgiven for his
        name's sake.

I am writing to you, fathers,

> because you know him who is from the
> beginning.

I am writing to you, young men,

> because you have overcome the evil one.

I write to you, children,

> because you know the Father.

I write to you, fathers,

> because you know him who is from the
> beginning.

I write to you, young men,

> because you are strong,
> and the word of God abides in you,
> and you have overcome the evil one. (1 John
> 2:12–14 ESV)

When I was a child, I spoke like a child, I thought like a child, I reasoned like a child. When I became a man, I gave up childish ways. (1 Cor. 13:11 ESV)

During this stage, Jesus does His marvelous work of transformation by His Spirit (Rom. 12:1–2). Transformation points to the Lord's role in allowing us to go through trials and tribulations, which are designed to work His character into us. This is the experiential side of the cross.

From a parent's perspective, it is difficult to watch our children go through this maturing process. Frustration produces growth, but we don't want our children bouncing from one failure to another. However, parents who don't allow their kids to risk, stumble, and fall are actually stunting their children's growth.

> Consider it all joy, my brethren, when you encounter various trials, knowing that the testing of your faith produces endurance. And let endurance have its perfect result, so that you may be perfect and complete, lacking in nothing. (James 1:2–4)

> You greatly rejoice [in your salvation], even though now for a little while, if necessary, you have been distressed by various trials, so that the proof of your faith, being more precious than gold which is perishable, even though tested by fire, may be found to result in praise and glory and honor at the revelation of Jesus Christ. (1 Pet. 1:6–7; see also 1 Pet. 4:12–13)

> We also exult in our tribulations, knowing that tribulation brings about perseverance; and

perseverance, proven character; and proven
character, hope. (Rom. 5:3–4)

Jesus' present-day ministry of reproving and disciplining us
is also included in this stage:

> Those whom I love, I reprove and discipline;
> therefore be zealous and repent. (Rev. 3:19)

> But when we are judged, we are disciplined
> by the Lord so that we will not be condemned
> along with the world. (1 Cor. 11:32)

Discipline versus Condemnation

Some who hold to an error-by-emphasis perspective concerning grace ignore the fact that Jesus disciplines us and the Father
chastens us. Their thinking is, *If Jesus forgave all my sin and I'm
not condemned, how could He discipline and chastise me?*

But the Scripture plainly states that He does. Imagine a
father who says the following of his toddler:

> My daughter will always be my blood kin.
> I will always unconditionally accept her,
> and she will always be related to me. I will

never disown her, no matter what she does. I'm related to her by blood. That will never change. In fact, I love her so much that she's already forgiven, despite the wrong things that she will do in life and the mistakes she will make. But when my daughter does something wrong, there are consequences. I discipline her. Why? Because I have a duty to train her to do good, and I want her to mend any relationship she damages.

It's the same way with God. He unconditionally accepts us. He is our Father, and we are His children. That doesn't change. In addition, because of Jesus' shed blood, He forgave us long before we ever screwed up. But because He is our Father and He loves us, He will chasten us when we repeatedly act contrary to our new nature in Him. And Jesus will discipline us. This isn't condemnation; it's loving correction. It may not feel good, but sometimes love doesn't feel good.

Point: Just because you and I are forgiven by the blood of Christ for all our sins—past, present, and future—this doesn't mean there are no consequences to our actions. It doesn't mean the Spirit cannot be grieved. It doesn't mean the Spirit cannot be quenched. And it doesn't mean the Lord cannot be displeased with a particular act or attitude we adopt.

God can unconditionally accept us while still disciplining us, because we are His much-loved children. Remember, His ultimate goal is to confirm us to the image of Jesus, His Son (Rom. 8:28–29):

> Endure hardship as discipline; God is treating you as his children. For what children are not disciplined by their father? If you are not disciplined—and everyone undergoes discipline—then you are not legitimate, not true sons and daughters at all. Moreover, we have all had human fathers who disciplined us and we respected them for it. How much more should we submit to the Father of spirits and live! They disciplined us for a little while as they thought best; but God disciplines us for our good, in order that we may share in his holiness. No discipline seems pleasant at the time, but painful. Later on, however, it produces a harvest of righteousness and peace for those who have been trained by it. (Heb. 12:7–11 NIV)

The Human Conscience

I want to explore the human conscience and its role in our walk with God in a bit more depth here than I did in chapter 1.

Think of the conscience as a window by which the light of heaven shines through to our spirits. Through the conscience, the Holy Spirit corrects, reprimands, and makes us feel uneasy when we take a step that contradicts our new nature in Christ.

A believer's conscience reproves sin and approves righteousness. In order to walk in the Spirit, we must learn how to be sensitive to the voice of our consciences. For the Christian, the conscience is an inward monitor that alerts us to our spiritual condition.

The conscience bears witness to God's will (Rom. 2:15; 2 Cor. 4:2), and it testifies to the truth (Rom. 9:1; 2 Cor. 1:12; 5:11). Paul and Peter exhorted believers to follow their consciences (Rom. 13:5; 1 Cor. 10:25–29; 1 Pet. 2:19).

The New Testament describes five different states of the human conscience:

1. A cleansed or purified conscience (Heb. 9:9, 14). A conscience that has been cleansed from guilt and protest by the blood of Christ.

2. A good, blameless, or clear conscience (Acts 23:1; 24:16; 1 Tim. 1:5, 19; 3:9; 2 Tim. 1:3; Heb. 13:18; 1 Pet. 3:16, 21). A conscience that is free from guilt, protestation, or reprimand. A believer is walking

in the Spirit and the dictates of his or her conscience. As a result, the believer has unclouded communion with God. There is no stain on the window, so God's light can easily penetrate into their spirits.

3. An evil or defiled conscience (Titus 1:15; Heb. 10:22). A conscience that protests that a person is violating God's will in his or her behavior or attitude.

4. A seared conscience (1 Tim. 4:2). A conscience whose correction and protest has been ignored and suppressed. The individual has quenched and deadened the voice of his or her conscience.

5. A weak conscience (1 Cor. 8:7–12). A conscience that has been misinformed that some things are wrong for a particular individual when they are permissible for others (Paul used the examples of eating meat and drinking wine in Romans 14 and 1 Corinthians 8).

It's all too easy to hang on to a sinful attitude or practice and ignore the dictates of one's conscience. I know, because I've done this myself in my foolishness.

If we will walk in the Spirit, then, we would be wise to let our consciences probe our lives, let them expose our faults, and accept their reprimands. Doing so is to deal with any sin in our lives by applying the blood of Christ, which cleanses our consciences, and repenting so that we may break free from sin's consequences. In this way, the clouds that cover over the window of our consciences can be removed, and God's light can shine through without hindrance.

The fact is, the more closely we walk with God, the more keenly alert we will be to the inward monitor of our consciences.

The Shaper and the Shape

Jesus is both the shape and the shaper—the former and the form—as He works Himself into us, conforming us into His glorious image. Specifically ...

- He manifests His life through our bodies (2 Cor. 4:10–11).
- He makes His home in our hearts (Eph. 3:17).
- He becomes wisdom, righteousness, sanctification, and redemption to us (1 Cor. 1:30).
- He makes us stand (Rom. 14:4).
- He directs our way (1 Thess. 3:11).
- He directs our hearts into His love (2 Thess. 3:5).

- He gives us understanding (2 Tim. 2:7).
- He reveals to us what is proper (Philem. v. 8).
- He stands with us and strengthens us (2 Tim. 4:17).
- He examines us (1 Cor. 4:4).
- He protects us from the Evil One (2 Thess. 3:3).
- He causes us to "increase and abound" in our love for others (1 Thess. 3:12).
- He establishes our hearts (1 Thess. 3:13).
- He grants peace in every circumstance (2 Thess. 3:16).
- He demonstrates His perfect patience in our lives (1 Tim. 1:16).
- He delivers us from this present evil age (Gal. 1:4).
- He delivers us from every evil deed and will bring us safely into His kingdom (2 Tim. 4:18).
- He redeems and purifies us (Titus 1:14).
- He is not ashamed to call us His kin (Heb. 2:11).
- He atones for our sins (Heb. 2:17).
- He comes to our aid in times of temptation (Heb. 2:18; 4:14–16).
- He builds His house, of which we are a part (Heb. 3:3).

• He knows how to rescue the godly out of temptation (2 Pet. 3:9).

As we grow into Christ, we move from childhood to adulthood. The Bible describes this stage of maturity as attaining
our full stature in Christ:

> Until we all attain to the unity of the faith
> and of the knowledge of the Son of God,
> to mature manhood, to the measure of the
> stature of the fullness of Christ, so that we
> may no longer be children, tossed to and fro
> by the waves and carried about by every wind
> of doctrine, by human cunning, by craftiness
> in deceitful schemes. Rather, speaking the
> truth in love, we are to grow up in every way
> into him who is the head, into Christ. (Eph.
> 4:13–15 ESV)

> Though by this time you ought to be teach-
> ers, you need someone to teach you again the
> basic principles of the oracles of God. You need
> milk, not solid food, for everyone who lives on
> milk is unskilled in the word of righteousness,
> since he is a child. (Heb. 5:12–13 ESV)

> Therefore let us leave the elementary doctrine of
> Christ and go on to maturity, not laying again a
> foundation of repentance from dead works and
> of faith toward God, and of instruction about
> washings, the laying on of hands, the resurrec-
> tion of the dead, and eternal judgment. And
> this we will do if God permits. (Heb. 6:1–3 ESV)

There is another term that the New Testament uses to describe this stage of spiritual maturity. The word is *adoption*.

Adoption in the New Testament is different from adoption today. The New Testament authors spoke of adoption as "sonship."

A child in the first century was no different from a servant. During the long period of child training and preparation for full sonship, a tutor would bring the child into the methods, intentions, and spirit of the child's father. Thus adoption was the *placing* of one who was already a child into full sonship rights.

Consequently, *adoption* is not a word of relationship but of position. You as a Christian are a child of God by new birth. But adoption is God's act in which you are placed in the position of an adult son (Gal. 4:1–5).

Greek, Roman, and Jewish families adopted their own children. Birth made them children, but discipline and training brought them into adoption and the full stature of sonship.

Simply put, *a child has God's nature, but a son has God's character.*

Children are born of God; sons are taught of God. Note that in the New Testament, "sons" and "brethren" also include women.

God desires to bring "many sons to glory" (Heb. 2:10). And He wants those sons (which includes His daughters) to be "built together" as a living temple (Eph. 2:20–22). Thus relatedness to other members of the body is essential for growth into Christ.

Advice for New Christians

The beginning of the Christian life is easy. The end is joyous. But the middle is where the fiercest battles take place, and many fall away.

The real test of faith comes in the middle of our journey. Jesus is the trailblazer, pathfinder, and pilgrim of God's way. This is the meaning of Christ being the pioneer and perfecter of our faith.

Not only did Jesus blaze the trail, but He also finished the pilgrimage. And He gives His people the strength to tread where He trod and arrive where He awaits.

Therefore, since we have so great a cloud of witnesses surrounding us, let us also lay aside

every encumbrance and the sin which so easily entangles us, and let us run with endurance
the race that is set before us, fixing our eyes
on Jesus, the author and perfecter of faith, who
for the joy set before Him endured the cross,
despising the shame, and has sat down at the
right hand of the throne of God.

For consider Him who has endured such
hostility by sinners against Himself, so that you
will not grow weary and lose heart. (Heb. 12:1–3)

I wish someone had told me the following things when I
was walking on the clouds of the newfound joy of my salvation
at age sixteen.

This list goes beyond the typical recommendations for
new believers (read the Bible, pray regularly, get involved
in a fellowship, etc.). I'm not mentioning those, as they are
"givens."

The list doesn't represent any kind of order or priority.
Rather, this list offers some honest insights and practical advice
for your journey as a believer:

- Christians will break your heart. The greatest
  pain you will receive will be at the hands of
  fellow and professing believers.

- Not everyone who professes Christ knows Him. The fruit of real faith is love—treating all others the same way you want to be treated.

- God will not meet all of your expectations and will sometimes appear not to fulfill His own promises.

- You will experience dry spells where there is no sense of God's presence. Learn to live by faith, not feelings.

- Build a library and read the best Christian books in print. Don't waste your time on "pop" Christian books. Go for depth.

- Write your goals down (goals = dreams = prayer requests). And document when a prayer or goal is answered or fulfilled.

- Never judge other Christians unless you've walked in their shoes. Always think the best of others (Matt. 7:12).

- Choose a mentor, but never choose one who is insecure, speaks negatively about others, or has an inflated ego.

- Some of the things you struggle with now you will struggle with when you are old. Resist condemnation (Rom. 8:1).

- Many of the answers you have now will prove inadequate later in life. Always be a student and a child in the kingdom.
- Never bluff an answer to someone's biblical or theological question if you don't know the answer. Learn to say, "I don't know."
- Discover who you are in Christ and learn what it means to live by His indwelling life.

Our Glorifier

There will come a time when Jesus will glorify us and give us a body just like His. This phenomenon is called glorification.

Glorification is the highest expression of a life. When a flower comes into full bloom, it is glorified. In the words of deeper-Christian-life writer Andrew Murray, "To glorify is to manifest the hidden excellence and worth of an object."[1]

There will come a day when Jesus will manifest our sonship (and daughtership) to the world. He will give us a resurrected, glorified body just like His. The seed of God's life that first entered into us will have grown into its fullest and highest potential:

---

1   Andrew Murray, *The Spirit of Christ* (London: James Nisbet, 1888), 106.

[He] will transform our lowly body to be like his glorious body, by the power that enables him even to subject all things to himself. (Phil. 3:21 ESV)

Those whom he predestined he also called, and those whom he called he also justified, and those whom he justified he also glorified. (Rom. 8:30 ESV)

So will it be with the resurrection of the dead. The body that is sown is perishable, it is raised imperishable; it is sown in dishonor, it is raised in glory; it is sown in weakness, it is raised in power; it is sown a natural body, it is raised a spiritual body. (1 Cor. 15:42–44 NIV)

Beloved, now we are children of God, and it has not appeared as yet what we will be. We know that when He appears, we will be like Him, because we will see Him just as He is. (1 John 3:2)

This is all part of Jesus' present-day ministry. It is to perfect what He started in us.

From Center to Circumference

Contrary to popular opinion, spiritual growth does not take place from the outside in. It works from the inside out.

You see, when you repent and believe upon Christ, He comes into you as a seed. That is, His own uncreated, divine life takes up residence inside your deepest being. You are given the indwelling life of Christ by the Holy Spirit.

And as you grow, the seed of His life begins to spread, seeking to dominate your soul (your mind, will, and emotions). This is what transformation is all about. And eventually the seed of God's life will dominate your entire body (glorified).

So the crucial element of transformation and discipleship is learning how to live by the indwelling life of Christ. Jesus is our model for living the Christian life. But how did He live it?

He didn't live it by any external means. Rather, He lived by His Father's indwelling life.

When Christ rose from the dead and ascended to heaven, He returned in the Spirit to live His life in and through His people. So the passage moved from the Father to the Son, from the Son to us.

Jesus Christ is now our indwelling Lord.[2]

---

2   I deal with this topic practically in my online discipleship course "Living by the Indwelling Life of Christ." You can access the course at TheDeeperJourney.com.

While there is a great deal of talk today about following Jesus and being a disciple, very little airtime has been given to discovering how to live by Christ's indwelling life. This is both tragic and ironic because we cannot follow Jesus or properly be His disciple if we don't know how to live by His life.

Pleasing God

In chapter 1 we talked about God's complete acceptance of us based upon the shed blood of His Son. If you've turned away from living a life of independence from God (repentance) and you've entrusted your life to Jesus as Lord and Savior (faith), then you are in Christ, and God unconditionally accepts you as holy, blameless, and without flaw.

However, as far as your conduct goes, God can be pleased or displeased.

Consider a father who loves his children. His love and acceptance of each child never changes, despite the poor decisions they may make in life.

Yet even though the father accepts and loves each child, some of his children may please him, while others may displease him.

This is an important distinction to make.

Love and acceptance are unconditional in Christ, but pleasing God is based on our choices.

Following are a number of texts in the New Testament that give us insight into what pleases God. May they encourage and inspire you.

> Those who are in the flesh cannot please God. (Rom. 8:8 ESV)

> I have received full payment, and more. I am well supplied, having received from Epaphroditus the gifts you sent, a fragrant offering, a sacrifice acceptable and pleasing to God. (Phil. 4:18 ESV)

> Children, obey your parents in everything, for this pleases the Lord. (Col. 3:20 ESV)

> First of all, then, I urge that supplications, prayers, intercessions, and thanksgivings be made for all people, for kings and all who are in high positions, that we may lead a peaceful and quiet life, godly and dignified in every way. This is good, and it is pleasing in the sight of God our Savior. (1 Tim. 2:1–3 ESV)

> Without faith it is impossible to please him, for whoever would draw near to God must believe

that he exists and that he rewards those who
seek him. (Heb. 11:6 ESV)

Do not neglect to do good and to share what
you have, for such sacrifices are pleasing to
God. (Heb. 13:16 ESV)

Becoming What You Already Are

As I put it in *Revise Us Again*, spiritual growth is a matter of
becoming what you already are. As a Christian, you are already
"Light in the Lord." Because this is true, Paul exhorted us to
"walk as children of Light" (Eph. 5:8).

In Ephesians, Paul said two times to "speak the truth in
love" to one another (4:15, 25). In context, Paul was exhorting
God's people to remind one another of who they were in Christ
… to remind one another about the new self into which they
had been made … to remind one another of their true identity.
Because it's all too easy to forget.

If you have received Jesus Christ as Savior and Lord, here's
a list of who you *really* are. Read this list carefully and marvel at
the epic greatness of your Lord and what He has done for you:

- You are complete in Christ, "who is the head
of all principality and power" (Col. 2:10 NKJV).

- You have been "crucified with Christ" (Gal. 2:20).
- You are dead to sin (Rom. 6:2).
- You have been made "alive with Christ" (Eph. 2:5 NIV).
- You are "free from the law of sin and death" (Rom. 8:2).
- You are born of God, and the Evil One does not touch you (1 John 5:18).
- You are holy and without blame before Him in love (Eph. 1:4; see also 1 Pet. 1:16).
- You have been given the peace of God that passes all understanding (Phil. 4:7).
- You have the Greater One living in you; "greater is He who is in you than he who is in the world" (1 John 4:4).
- You have received the "gift of righteousness" and "reign in life" by Jesus Christ (Rom. 5:17).
- You have received the "spirit of wisdom and of revelation in the knowledge of Jesus" (Eph. 1:17–18).
- You can do all things through Christ Jesus, who strengthens you (Phil. 4:13).
- You show forth "the praises of God," who has "called you out of darkness into His marvellous light" (1 Pet. 2:9 KJV).

- You are God's child, born again of the incorruptible seed of the Word of God (1 Pet. 1:23 KJV; see also John 1:12).
- You are God's masterpiece, "created in Christ Jesus unto good works" (Eph. 2:10 KJV).
- You are a "new creature" in Christ (2 Cor. 5:17).
- You are "alive to God" (Rom. 6:11).
- You are an heir of God and a joint heir with Christ (Rom. 8:17 NKJV).
- You are more than a conqueror through Him who loves you (Rom. 8:37).
- You have been brought near to God by the blood of Christ (Eph. 2:13).
- You are beloved of God (1 John 4:10).
- You are loved by the Father the same way Jesus is loved by the Father (John 17:23).
- You have been redeemed from "the curse of the law" (Gal. 3:13).
- You have been "freed from all things" (Acts 13:39).
- You are now God's offspring (1 John 3:2).
- "You are the salt of the earth" (Matt. 5:13).
- You have been reconciled to God (2 Cor. 5:18).

- You have been accepted by God in the beloved Son (Eph. 1:6).
- You are kept by the power of God (1 Cor. 1:8).
- You are free in Christ (John 8:36; Gal. 5:1).
- You are in Christ's hands, out of which no one can snatch you (John 10:28).
- You are in the Father's hands, out of which no one can snatch you (John 10:29).
- You are an overcomer by "the blood of the Lamb" and the word of your testimony (Rev. 12:11).
- You are a partaker of God's divine nature (2 Pet. 1:3–4).
- You are part of "a chosen generation, a royal priesthood, a holy nation," a purchased people (1 Pet. 2:9 NKJV).
- You are "the righteousness of God" in Christ Jesus (2 Cor. 5:21).
- You are "a temple of the Holy Spirit" (1 Cor. 6:19).
- "You are the light of the world" (Matt. 5:14).
- You are God's elect, full of mercy, kindness, humility, and longsuffering (Rom. 8:33; Col. 3:12).
- You are forgiven of all sins and washed in the blood (Eph. 1:7).

- You have been delivered from the power of darkness and translated into God's kingdom (Col. 1:13 KJV).

- You have "put off the old man" and have "put on the new man" (Col. 3:9–10 NKJV).

- You are healed by the "stripes" of Jesus (1 Pet. 2:24 NKJV).

- You are raised up with Christ and seated in "heavenly places" (Eph. 2:6; Col. 2:12).

- You have "overcome the world" (1 John 5:4).

- You are greatly loved by God (Rom. 1:7; Eph. 2:4; Col. 3:12; 1 Thess. 1:4).

- You are "strengthened with all power according to His glorious might" (Col. 1:11).

- You have not been given "a spirit of fear, but of power, and of love, and of a sound mind" (2 Tim. 1:7 NKJV).

- You have Christ living inside of you (Gal. 2:20).

- You are a saint—a holy one (Col. 1:2).

- You are "one spirit" with the Lord (1 Cor. 6:17).

- You are holy, without reproof, and blameless in His sight (Col. 1:22).

- You are a member of Christ's holy body (1 Cor. 12:27).
- You have been given "all things that pertain to life and godliness" (2 Pet. 1:3 NKJV).
- "You are Light in the Lord" (Eph. 5:8).
- You have been given "every spiritual blessing in the heavenly places in Christ" (Eph. 1:3).
- You were chosen in Christ "before the foundation of the world" (Eph. 1:4).
- You have been justified by faith—just as if you had never sinned (Rom. 5:1).
- You are a branch on the "true vine" (John 15:1, 5).
- You are "born of God" (1 John 5:18).
- You have direct access to the "throne of grace" through Jesus Christ (Heb. 4:14–16).
- You are free from condemnation, and you cannot be charged or indicted (Rom. 8:1, 32–34).
- You have been established, anointed, and sealed by God (2 Cor. 1:21–22).
- You are "hidden with Christ in God" (Col. 3:1–4).
- You are a citizen of heaven (Phil. 3:20).
- You are at peace with God (Rom. 5:1).

- You have "everlasting life" (John 5:24 NKJV).
- You are kept by God's power (1 Pet. 1:5).
- You are in Christ Jesus by God's act (1 Cor. 1:30).
- You cannot be separated from God's love in Christ (Rom. 8:35–39).
- You are fit to partake of His inheritance (Col. 1:12 NKJV; Eph. 1:14).
- You are part of Christ's bride, whom He cherishes, bone of His bone and flesh of His flesh (Eph. 5:29–32 NKJV).
- You are a king and priest to God (Rev. 1:6 NKJV).
- You have been sealed with the promised Holy Spirit until the day of redemption (Eph. 1:13; 4:30).
- God will complete the good work that He started in you (Phil. 1:6).
- God is for you even when others are against you (Rom. 8:31).

Jesus is our Savior. On the grounds of His death, burial, resurrection, and ascension, He saves us from the penalty of sin; He saves us from the power of sin; and He will ultimately save us from the presence of sin.

As our Savior, He saves us "to the uttermost" (Heb. 7:25 ESV) and will complete in us what He began. Indeed, He is the originator and perfecter of our faith.

CHAPTER 5

BUILDER OF *EKKLESIA*

Upon this rock I will build My church; and the
gates of Hades will not overpower it.

Matthew 16:18

Imagine that a friend of yours buys a house in your neighborhood. He lives just down the street from you, and you visit his house frequently. The house looks great to you. But then something happens one day that takes you aback. Construction crews show up and launch an entire home remodel. This is surprising because your friend's house was absolutely fine just the way it was, or so you thought.

You watch as fine cabinets are replaced with different ones, doors are pulled out, and windows are recut. You observe walls being shifted and flooring being peeled back and laid down differently.

Why? Because, even though all that existing material was *good*, it wasn't according to your friend's ultimate vision for a house. So it wasn't really useful. As the owner of the house, your friend didn't care how good or decent something was—he was only interested in building according to his vision. And rightly so, because the house belongs to him.

This story applies to the Christian life. If we read Scripture carefully, we discover that God has been working on a building project since before the foundation of the universe. And He is totally committed to completing it according to His heavenly vision and eternal purpose.

As we discover more about God in Christ as a wise master builder, we find this truth everywhere. Consider that the first and most important result of Christ's ascension is the birth of the *ekklesia*.

Mark tells us that after His ascension, Jesus "worked with" the apostles and "confirmed" the Word with signs (Mark 16:20).

For what reason? *To build His* ekklesia *on earth*.

Hebrews tells us that not only is Jesus Christ our high priest, but He's also our apostle—*the builder* of His house:

> Therefore, holy brothers and sisters, who share
> in the heavenly calling, fix your thoughts on

Jesus, whom we acknowledge as our apostle and high priest. He was faithful to the one who appointed him, just as Moses was faithful in all God's house. Jesus has been found worthy of greater honor than Moses, just as the builder of a house has greater honor than the house itself. For every house is built by someone, but God is the builder of everything. (3:1–4 NIV)

The Lord Jesus builds His *ekklesia* by two means: (1) by calling some of His servants to plant His church and equip the saints, and (2) by endowing His people with spiritual giftings.

In that connection, I'm often asked, "Do you believe in the fivefold ministry? And do you believe that God is restoring it today?" I'll answer those questions in this chapter, because they have everything to do with how Jesus builds His *ekklesia* today. Please consider my remarks in the context of the story I told at the beginning of this chapter and the larger truths I've been presenting in this book.

Our God isn't so interested in remote and ideological doctrines that are more true than useful. He's committed to a heavenly building plan, and He is working accordingly. Our Lord is more interested in functionality than form.

My answer largely hinges on what one means by the "fivefold ministry." In other words, what fivefold ministry are we talking about? Are we talking about the two-hundred-year-old doctrine of the restoration of the "fivefold ministry"? Or are we talking about the ascension gifts that Paul had in mind when he penned Ephesians 4:9–16?

The Making of a Doctrine

In nineteenth-century England, Christians were ripe to embrace apocalyptic prophecies about the coming millennial age. The upheaval that the French Revolution produced left God's people wishing for a reign of peace that would set all things right.

In 1824, Edward Irving, a Presbyterian pastor in Scotland, began teaching that the fivefold ministry of apostles, prophets, evangelists, pastors, and teachers had disappeared from the church and was in need of restoration. According to Irving, the restoration of these ministries would usher in the millennial kingdom of Christ on the earth.

Irving and his followers began the Catholic Apostolic Church in 1832. Its chief purpose was to restore the fivefold ministry and usher in the millennial kingdom. The church ordained twelve "apostles," who were to be the last days' equivalent of the original Twelve whom Jesus appointed. Henry Drummond, a wealthy banker from England, became the leader of the church. Drummond himself took the highest position—"apostle to Scotland."

It was prophesied that these twelve apostles would be the last apostles to appear on earth before Christ's return. (This is a throwback to Mani of Persia of the third century, who labeled himself the Apostle of Light and the very last apostle of Jesus.)

Eventually the twelve apostles of the Catholic Apostolic Church died (the last one died in 1901). Upon their death, the CAC expired in England. In Germany, however, the CAC ordained twelve more apostles and took the name of the New Apostolic Church.

In 1896, an erstwhile Congregational minister named John Alexander Dowie founded the Christian Catholic Church. In 1901, with five thousand followers, Dowie established the city of Zion in northeast Illinois. In 1904, Dowie announced that he had been divinely commissioned to be the first apostle. He then told his followers to anticipate the full restoration of apostolic Christianity. In 1906, the community of believers in the city of Zion began to break down. Dowie passed away the following year.

Following the famed Azusa Street revival in 1906 in Los Angeles, California, the emphasis on the restoration of the five-fold ministry and "a mighty outpouring of the Holy Spirit just before the return of Christ" reappeared. And a new generation of apostles emerged. Luigi Francescon ("apostle to Italy"), Ivan Voronaev ("apostle to the Slavs"), and T. B. Barratt ("apostle to Europe") were just some of them.

Pentecostal denominations in Wales, New Zealand, Australia, Canada, and the United States elected and ordained colleges of apostles to govern their denominations.

As the years rolled on, the restoration of the fivefold-ministry doctrine somewhat faded. But it reemerged with a revival spawned at Sharon Orphanage in North Battleford, Saskatchewan, Canada, in 1948. The New Order of the Latter Rain movement, as it was called, was prophesied to restore the fivefold ministry to prepare for "the manifestation of the sons of God" on the earth.

But when the waters of revival receded, the restoration of the fivefold-ministry doctrine faded again until it was resuscitated in the Charismatic movement of the late 1960s. In the late seventies, the doctrine's flame began to dim again until a group of men resurrected it with new fervor in the mid-1990s.

In 1996, Peter Wagner led a conference at Fuller Theological Seminary titled the National Symposium on the Post-Denominational Church. This conference produced a new movement called the New Apostolic movement, which Wagner claimed was sweeping the globe with a new way of doing church. The churches that were part of this movement were labeled New Apostolic churches.

In 1999, Wagner sought to organize the movement as the International Coalition of Apostles, with Wagner as the presiding apostle. The movement claims to be restoring the fivefold ministry today.

Parenthetically, the churches in the New Apostolic movement are vanilla Charismatic churches where the pastor is often renamed "apostle."

Point: The doctrine of the restoration of the fivefold ministry is more than 180 years old. And it's been repackaged from movement to movement.

Running the Cart over the Horse

So is God going to restore the fivefold ministry? To my mind, that's the wrong question. It's pushing the cart before the horse. The ascension gifts mentioned in Ephesians 4 are anointed people whom God gives to the body of Christ. They are the natural outgrowth and by-product of organic church life.

All in all, there are twenty gifts mentioned in the New Testament. If a group of believers gathers around Jesus Christ alone (rather than a doctrine, a theological system, or a ritual)—and they are void of a clergy system—then that group will eventually produce all the gifts and gifted ones that exist within the body of Christ.

It's no mistake that Paul used the physical human body as an apt image to describe the way the body of Christ functions. When a baby girl is born, most of her capabilities are not present. She can't ride a bicycle, add and subtract numbers, or eat with a fork and knife.

However, within her body she possesses the genetic codes that will produce the physical development by which she'll one day carry out these activities. If she is fed and nurtured properly, in time these abilities will automatically develop within her without being forced or manufactured by other humans. She will organically grow into them. Why? Because they are native to her species as a human being. They are the product of human life.[1]

In the same way, when a genuine church is born, it possesses within its spiritual DNA all the giftings that are in Jesus Christ. But it takes time for them to develop and emerge. (Unfortunately, we live in a day when many church leaders don't seem to understand this spiritual principle. Hence, they try to force the exercise of gifts and ministries in the body prematurely.)

What is needed, then, is not a restoration of the so-called fivefold ministry. What's needed is the restoration of organic church life. And that is what God is seeking to restore today as He has in every generation.

Therefore, if we can discover how a church is born from God's perspective and how it is to be nurtured and maintained, then we will see a restoration of all the gifts that are in Christ *in the way* that they were meant to be expressed.

---

1   For details on the organic expression of the church, see my book *Reimagining Church*.

A Personal Testimony

Since I've been meeting in organic churches over the past twenty years, I've made a startling discovery: the gifts of the Holy Spirit function very differently in an organic expression of the church than they do in the typical institutional church. The gift of prophecy, for example, that comes up out of the soil of authentic body life looks profoundly different from the way it's packaged in the typical Pentecostal/Charismatic church. (The latter is often based on imitating others.)

In the 1980s I was part of a spontaneous expression of organic church life. Most of us who were gathering at that time came from the Pentecostal/Charismatic tradition. We functioned freely in spiritual gifts as they were modeled to us by that tradition. A number of years later, a group whose background was anti-Pentecostal/Charismatic joined us, and we had a first-class dilemma on our hands.

After a bloodletting church split, the Lord graciously showed us that both groups needed to lay down their beliefs and practice of spiritual gifts and leave them at the foot of the cross. Though it was difficult, we let our ideas and practice of the gifts go into death.

In a year's time, something remarkable happened. The gifts of the Holy Spirit were resurrected in our gatherings. However, they looked very different from what any of us had ever seen before. The Pentecostal/Charismatic packaging was utterly stripped away. And what was left was a pure expression of the Holy Spirit that glorified, unveiled, and lifted up the Lord Jesus Christ. As a result, the two groups came into a unified experience of the Holy Spirit's power and work.

Consequently, the pressing question is, are we going to get serious about discovering how to gather around Jesus Christ in an organic way? Or are we going to blithely ignore New Testament principles, and for the next two hundred years continue to hope (and prophesy) that the fivefold ministry will one day be restored?

Again, God's way of raising up the ascension gifts is by restoring organic body life. The ascension gifts don't magically appear because someone writes a book prophesying that they're just around the corner. Nor should we assume that they have been restored when someone claims to be the "first," the "last," or the "new" apostle.

Authentic apostles, prophets, evangelists, and shepherds/teachers are gifted people who grow up in organic churches—not as leaders but as brethren—equal in status to everyone else in the church. Because they have grown up out of the soil of authentic church life, they have been tested and proven to be safe to the kingdom of God and to the Lord's children.

Their outstanding hallmark is that they glorify, reveal, present, magnify, and bring into clear view the Lord Jesus Christ in unusual depths and practical experience.

This is the heritage of the Ephesians 4 ascension gifts. It was true for all the apostles, prophets, evangelists, and shepherds/teachers in the first century. And Jesus Christ has not changed (Heb. 13:8).

The Peril of a Wrong Environment

So what happens when gifted Christians are reared in a human organization built on unbiblical systems rather than in an organic expression of the body of Christ? To put it another way, what happens when a gifted Christian's only experience is in the modern institutional church?

The answer? Mixture with a capital *M*.

Add to that a footnote: malfunction.

What happens when you remove polar bears from their natural habitat? If they survive (and some do not), they cannot function as God designed. They lose their ability to reproduce.

What happens when lions are caged and domesticated from birth? They lose their predatory and killer instincts. They lose something of the natural functioning with which God wired them.

Over the past decade, I've met scores of men who were self-proclaimed prophets and apostles. Some were genuinely gifted. Some had the gift of teaching. Others had authentic gifts of healing. Others had a genuine operation of the word of knowledge.

But most lacked any real depth in Christ and had very little experience in embracing His cross. And few of them grasped God's eternal purpose or witnessed real, thriving, healthy organic church life.

Why is this? Because of the institution that raised them up. Or in some cases, because they raised themselves up in isolation from other Christians. (The latter is an equally abnormal environment for a Christian to be nurtured in.)

To put it in a sentence, such men didn't grow up in their proper habitat. Few if any of them grew up in organic body life where they were simply brothers among other brothers.

Few if any spent any time in a New Testament expression of church life, where their weaknesses and blind spots were exposed to others. Instead, most were part of several institutional churches and launched out into independent ministry on their own.

As Watchman Nee once observed, "The tragedy in Christian work today is that so many of the workers have simply *gone* out, they have not been sent."[2]

The New Testament never envisions such a situation.

---

2   Watchman Nee, *The Finest of the Wheat*, vol. 2 (New York: Christian Fellowship Publishers, 1993), 511.

So What Are the Ascension Gifts?

When the ascension gifts emerge organically in a local assembly, their chief function is to nurture and encourage the believing community toward spiritual maturity in Christ, unity, and every-member functioning.

I will now try to demystify the so-called fivefold ministry and discuss how each of the ascension gifts probably functioned in the first century:

> *Apostles.* Apostles were extra-local, itinerant church planters. They were highly gifted individuals who were sent by the Lord and by a particular church to plant, build, and equip new churches. Paul, an apostle, referred to himself as a master builder (1 Cor. 3:10) as well as a planter (vv. 6–9).
>
> Apostles enabled the churches by giving them life, raising them up from the ground. They also helped them walk on their own two feet. Apostles grew up in an organic expression of church life. They were nonleaders before they were sent out to plant churches of the same kind. *In other words, they first experienced what they would later establish elsewhere.* And they

always left the churches they planted under the headship of Christ, without human control, even before elders and overseers emerged.

Prophets. Prophets were people who had a clear vision of Jesus Christ and were able to articulate it lucidly. Prophets enabled the church by speaking the present word of the Lord to it. Sometimes their words would simply reveal Christ to encourage, inspire, and comfort. Other times their words would cast spiritual vision. Prophets sought to restore God's will whenever it had been lost. They sometimes confirmed the gifts and callings of other members and prepared the church for future trials.

Evangelists. Evangelists enabled the church by modeling the preaching of the good news to the lost. They were fearless souls who possessed an extraordinary boldness to share Christ with nonbelievers. And they had a genuine passion for the unsaved. The closest equivalent to an evangelist today is a natural-born salesman (an honest one, of course).

Shepherds/teachers. Shepherds/teachers are two sides of the same gift. In Ephesians 4:11, the apostles, prophets, and evangelists are mentioned separately, while shepherds and teachers are joined together. Further, the first three ministries (apostles, prophets, and evangelists) are preceded by the word *some*. But the word *some* is attached to shepherds and teachers together. This indicates that shepherds/teachers are one gift.

The chief task of the shepherds/teachers was to help the church in times of personal crisis (shepherding) and to enlighten and cultivate the church's spiritual life by revealing Christ through the exposition of Scripture (teaching). Shepherding was the private side of their ministry; teaching was the public side. The closest equivalent to a first-century shepherd/teacher is a modern-day Christian counselor who is capable of teaching.

None of the ascension gifts dominated the meetings of the church. They were simply brothers and sisters in the body who carried out certain functions. Every other member functioned in the gatherings and in the community life of the church. In that connection, you would never see a first-century Christian sporting titles like "Apostle Delaquarius Epps," "Prophetess Teresa Thomas," or "Evangelist Fielding Melish." As I've

established elsewhere, the use of honorific titles and offices was
unknown to the early Christians.

The Spirit of Christ

Throughout the New Testament, the Holy Spirit is called by
the following names:

- The Spirit of God
- The Spirit of Christ
- The Spirit of the Father
- The Spirit of the Lord
- The Spirit of truth
- The Spirit of life in Christ Jesus
- The Spirit of holiness
- The Spirit of Him who raised Jesus from the
  dead
- The Spirit of the living God
- The Spirit of His Son
- The Spirit of Jesus Christ
- The Spirit of grace
- The Spirit of glory
- The Spirit of life
- The Comforter (which means advocate, coun-
  selor, or helper)

The Holy Spirit is the reality of Christ's presence. The Spirit dispenses to us the very life that Jesus lived.

At Pentecost, the Holy Spirit came as the Spirit of the glorified Christ, the Spirit of the incarnate, crucified, and exalted Jesus. Note that the risen Jesus didn't *become* the Holy Spirit. He rather came *in* the Spirit. Today, Jesus is present with us through the Spirit.

For this reason, the Holy Spirit is called the Spirit of Christ and the Spirit of Jesus (Rom. 8:9; 1 Pet. 1:11; Acts 16:7; Phil. 1:19). And Jesus is called a "life-giving spirit" (1 Cor. 15:45).

The continuing humanity of Christ in heaven is the guarantee of the new humanity that awaits every believer.

Because the Holy Spirit has been sent to earth, authentic humanity is now a reality made possible.

Ephesians 4 uses the images of descent and ascent. These terms remind us of the Old Testament high priest when he ascended the steps of the temple on the Day of Atonement for the forgiveness of sins. Then he descended to where the people were. Jesus ascends to heaven, and the Spirit descends to earth while Christ's throne is established at God's right hand.

Jesus ascended to the place from where He descended (John 3:13; 6:62; Eph. 4:10). Our eternal hope is found in His ascension, for He secured the glory for all who follow Him.

The incarnation was Jesus leaving God's space to enter man's space. The ascension was Jesus in His incarnation leaving man's space and going back to God's space.

The Lord Jesus Christ ascended into heaven in the same body in which He lived, was crucified, and rose again. Now, as a life-giving Spirit, Jesus communicates His life and presence to the members of His body across all realms, times, and distances (1 Cor. 15:45). Because Christ is now in the Spirit, Jesus and the Holy Spirit are sometimes spoken of interchangeably in the New Testament, even though the Spirit and the risen Christ are distinct persons (John 14–16; 2 Cor. 3:14–18).

The Holy Spirit is able to connect all believers to Christ. For this reason, Jesus said it was better for Him to go so that the Spirit could descend (John 7:39, John 16:5-15).

A careful look at John 14–16 reveals that Jesus would return again in the Spirit after He ascended. And He did so at Pentecost.

Fifty Things the Holy Spirit Does

- The Spirit convicts the world of sin, righteousness, and judgment (John 16:8).
- The Spirit guides us into all truth (John 16:13).
- The Spirit regenerates us (John 3:5–8; Titus 3:5).

- The Spirit glorifies and testifies of Christ (John 15:26; 16:14).
- The Spirit reveals Christ to us and in us (John 16:14–15).
- The Spirit leads us (Matt. 4:1; Luke 4:1; Rom. 8:14; Gal. 5:18).
- The Spirit sanctifies us (Rom. 15:16; 2 Thess. 2:13; 1 Pet. 1:2).
- The Spirit empowers us (Luke 4:14; 24:49; Acts 1:8; Rom. 15:19).
- The Spirit fills us (Acts 2:4; 4:8, 31; 9:17; Eph. 5:18).
- The Spirit teaches us to pray (Rom. 8:26-27; Jude 1:20).
- The Spirit "bears witness" in us "that we are children of God" (Rom. 8:16 NKJV).
- The Spirit produces in us the fruit or evidence of His work and presence (Gal. 5:22–23).
- The Spirit distributes spiritual gifts and manifestations (the outshining) of His presence to and through the body (1 Cor. 12:4, 8–10; Heb. 2:4).
- The Spirit anoints us for ministry (Luke 4:18; Acts 10:38).
- The Spirit washes and renews us (Titus 3:5).

- The Spirit brings unity and oneness to the body (Eph. 4:3; 2:14–18). Here He plays the same role that He plays in the Godhead. The Spirit is the life that unites Father and Son, and He plays this role in the church. When the Spirit is operating in a group of people, He unites them in love. Therefore, a sure evidence of the Holy Spirit working in a group is love and unity—not signs and wonders (those are seasonal and can be counterfeited).

- The Spirit is our guarantee and deposit of the future resurrection (2 Cor. 1:22; 5:5 NIV).

- The Spirit seals us for the day of redemption (Eph. 1:13; 4:30).

- The Spirit sets us "free from the law of sin and death" (Rom. 8:2).

- The Spirit quickens our mortal bodies (Rom. 8:11 KJV).

- The Spirit reveals "the deep things of God" to us (1 Cor. 2:10 NKJV).

- The Spirit reveals "what God has given us freely" (1 Cor. 2:12 NIV).

- The Spirit dwells in us (John 14:17; Rom. 8:9; 1 Cor. 3:16; 2 Tim. 1:14).

- The Spirit speaks to, in, and through us (Matt. 10:20; Acts 2:4; 8:29; 10:19; 11:12, 28; 13:2; 16:6, 7; 21:4, 11; 1 Cor. 12:3; 1 Tim. 4:1; Heb. 3:7; Rev. 2:11).
- The Spirit is the agent by which we are baptized into the body of Christ (1 Cor. 12:13).
- The Spirit brings liberty (2 Cor. 3:17).
- The Spirit transforms us into the image of Christ (2 Cor. 3:18).
- The Spirit cries in our hearts, "Abba! Father!" (Gal. 4:6).
- The Spirit enables us to wait (Gal. 5:5).
- The Spirit supplies us with Christ (Phil. 1:19 KJV).
- The Spirit grants everlasting life (Gal. 6:8 KJV).
- The Spirit gives us access to God the Father (Eph. 2:18).
- The Spirit makes us (corporately) God's habitation (Eph. 2:22 KJV).
- The Spirit reveals the mystery of God to us (Eph. 3:4–5).
- The Spirit strengthens our spirits (Eph. 3:16).
- The Spirit enables us to obey the truth (1 Pet. 1:22).

- The Spirit enables us to know that Jesus abides in us (1 John 3:24; 4:13).
- The Spirit confesses that Jesus came in the flesh (1 John 4:2).
- The Spirit says, "Come, Lord Jesus," along with the bride (Rev. 22:17).
- The Spirit pours out God's love into our hearts (Rom. 5:5).
- The Spirit bears witness to the truth in our conscience (Rom. 9:1).
- The Spirit teaches us (1 Cor. 2:13; John 14:26).
- The Spirit gives us joy (1 Thess. 1:6).
- The Spirit enables some to preach the gospel (1 Pet. 1:12).
- The Spirit moves us (2 Pet. 1:21).
- The Spirit knows the thoughts of God (1 Cor. 2:11).
- The Spirit casts out demons (Matt. 12:28).
- The Spirit brings things to our remembrance (John 14:26).
- The Spirit comforts us (Acts 9:31).
- The Spirit makes some overseers in the church, and through the body He sends some out to do the work of church planting (Acts 20:28; 13:2; 1 Cor. 1:17; Gal. 1:1).

In sum, the Holy Spirit unites us to Jesus Christ and to His body. He reveals Christ to us, gives us His life, and makes Christ alive in us.

The Spirit takes the experiences of Jesus—His incarnation, ministry, crucifixion, resurrection, and ascension—and brings them into our own experience. Because of the Holy Spirit, the history of Jesus Christ becomes our story and experience.

The Holy Spirit grants what Christ bestows. He makes real and experiential the work of Jesus. Therefore, we cannot separate what Christ does from what the Spirit does.

Charismania versus Charisphobia

In 1 Corinthians 12:7–10 (NKJV), Paul discussed the manifestation of the Holy Spirit, saying,

> But the manifestation of the Spirit is given to each one for the profit of all: for to one is given the word of wisdom through the Spirit, to another the word of knowledge through the same Spirit, to another faith by the same Spirit, to another gifts of healings by the same Spirit, to another the working of miracles, to another prophecy, to another discerning of spirits, to

another different kinds of tongues, to another
the interpretation of tongues.

As the name implies, the manifestation of the Holy Spirit
means that God gives the Spirit to *manifest*—to make known or
display—the presence of Jesus Christ to and through His church.

Since the Holy Spirit's job is to glorify and reveal Christ
(John 16:13–14), the manifestation of the Spirit is designed
to unveil Christ. Spiritual manifestations are given by God's
grace; consequently, Paul called them "spiritual gifts" (*charisma*
in the Greek; 1 Cor. 12:4, 30–31).

All nine gifts that Paul listed in the above text are miraculous
in nature. That is, they display Christ in a supernatural way.
Throughout the New Testament, Paul made a healthy distinction between the fruit of the Spirit and the gifts of the Spirit.

The fruit of the Spirit displays the *character* of God's life in
the believer. The manifestation of the Spirit displays the *power*
of God's life through the believer. The fruit of the Spirit relates
to our walk. The manifestation of the Spirit relates to our service. Fruit deals with the character of Jesus. Gifts deal with the
ministry of Jesus.

Spiritual manifestations have been a sore spot for the Lord's
people for centuries. Some have even embraced the notion that
those gifts are no longer present in the church.

Such folks are called "cessationists," for they believe that spiritual gifts have ceased to exist. But there is no biblical merit for the cessationist idea. The testimony of Scripture as well as church history demonstrate that the gifts of the Spirit have been operative in the church since they were given on the day of Pentecost in AD 30.

Nevertheless, among those who accept the perpetuity—or continuation—of spiritual manifestations, there have been two predominant schools of thought:

1. Spiritual gifts should be sought after and encouraged, for they are the zenith of spirituality.
2. Spiritual gifts should be hindered and discouraged, for they are easily abused and often cause division, confusion, and hurt.

I call the first view the *charismaniac* position and the second view the *charisphobic* position. I submit that both positions are imbalanced.

Gifts versus Life

A cardinal mistake that many believers make is to confuse spiritual gifts with spiritual life. God's highest aim for His children is that they grow and develop in spiritual life (1 Pet. 2:1–2).

As we grow in the life of Christ, we move closer to realizing the divine purpose of being conformed to the image of Jesus Christ (Rom. 8:28–29; 2 Cor. 3:18). We also begin to function in ministry. And effective functioning requires the exercise of spiritual gifts.

Stated simply, spiritual gifts are the tools by which we express spiritual life and spiritual power. Put another way, gifts are the utensils by which we supply spiritual food to others.

Now I ask you, which is more important—gift or life? Obviously, life is more important than gift, for food is more important than the utensil. Would it really matter if you were served a piece of steak with a spoon rather than a fork? Although it is easier to serve steak with a fork, the substance of what one is served is of greater significance than the utensil by which it is served.

While it is tragic to stress spiritual gifts over spiritual life, it is a grave mistake to stress spiritual life at the expense of spiritual gifts. Because of the overemphasis that some have placed on spiritual gifts and the abuses that have followed, some have opted to downplay and even ignore the role of spiritual gifts in the life of the church.

While spiritual gifts are certainly not a measure of spirituality, they are essential to the full expression of spiritual power and indispensable in spiritual service. To use a metaphor, we should not let the sloppy table manners of some prevent us from using the sanctified utensils that God makes available to us at His table.

Although the food may be more important than the utensil, it is a mistake to toss out the utensils. Note Paul's exhortation to the Corinthians to exercise spiritual gifts:

But *covet earnestly* the best gifts. (1 Cor. 12:31 KJV)

Desire earnestly spiritual gifts, but especially that you may prophesy. (1 Cor. 14:1)

Forasmuch as ye are *zealous* of spiritual gifts, *seek* that ye may excel to the edifying of the church. (1 Cor. 14:12 KJV)

How is it then, brethren? Whenever you come together, each of you has a psalm, has a teaching, has a tongue, has a revelation, has an interpretation. (1 Cor. 14:26 NKJV)

Covet to prophesy, and *forbid not* to speak with tongues. (1 Cor. 14:39 KJV)

Although the Corinthians were guilty of abusing spiritual gifts, Paul never told them to stop exercising them. Quite the contrary. Paul rebuked the Corinthians for their excesses. But he followed that rebuke with solid instruction on the proper use of the gifts. Paul's central point was that spiritual life (which is expressed through love) is to be preeminent over spiritual gifts (1 Cor. 13:1–8).

According to Paul, spiritual gifts ought always to be used for the sole purpose of edifying the body of Christ rather than ourselves. This is why Paul discussed the centrality and supremacy of love in 1 Corinthians 13 in the midst of his discourse on spiritual gifts in chapters 12 and 14. Gifts are to be governed by love for our brothers and sisters. They are to be used to build up the body in spiritual life.

Spiritual Manifestations

Beyond the gifts mentioned in Ephesians 4 (which are gifted people), Paul gave us another list of gifts in 1 Corinthians 12. These gifts are called "the manifestation of the Spirit" (v. 7).

These gifts aren't people but supernatural manifestations of the Holy Spirit whereby Jesus reveals Himself through the members of His body.

In order for us to understand the fullness of Christ's present-day ministry, we need to learn something about the manifestation of His Spirit in the church today.

I believe the "manifestation of the Spirit" can be divided into three categories: the revelatory gifts, the inspirational gifts, and the power gifts.

Note that these manifestations are different from other "gifts lists" in the New Testament (such as Romans 12) in that they are all supernatural in nature.

Note also that Jesus is the one who manifests Himself through these gifts by the operation of the Holy Spirit.

1. The Revelatory Gifts: Spiritual Manifestations of Disclosure

> *The word of knowledge.* The word of knowledge is a word from the Lord to the believer, revealing past or present facts in the mind of God.
>
> *The word of wisdom.* The word of wisdom is a word revealing God's purpose for the future (Luke 11:49).
>
> *The discerning of spirits.* The discerning—or distinguishing—of spirits enables one to perceive the spirit world.

2. The Inspirational Gifts: Spiritual Manifestations of Utterance

> *Prophecy.* To prophesy is to speak forth the present mind of the Lord.

Different kinds of tongues. Different (various) kinds of tongues are supernatural utterances in unknown languages.

The interpretation of tongues. The interpretation of tongues is the supernatural gift that enables one to interpret (not translate) an utterance given in other tongues.

3. The Power Gifts: Spiritual Manifestations of the Miraculous

The working of miracles. The working of miracles is the supernatural ability to manifest a divine intervention in the normal order of things.

Gifts of healing. This gift manifests divine healing in a person's body.

The gift of faith. The gift of faith is a special kind of faith that produces and receives the working of miracles.

Answering the Call

The burden of my heart is to see God's people far less concerned with a fivefold ministry and supernatural gifts that are supposed to be recovered someday, and instead focus their attention on discovering what the church is supposed to be according to the mind of God.

Upon making this discovery, the Lord's dear people will be faced with a decision: to answer the call of meeting around Jesus Christ alone in the way that He has prescribed, or to remain chained to the unmovable traditions of men.

If the former path is taken, it will involve considerable cost. But all the giftings in Christ will eventually come forth in the way that He has designed organically. And those gifts will never usurp or dilute the ministry of the entire body.

Would to God that all men and women who feel called to be apostles, prophets, evangelists, and shepherds/teachers would soberly reexamine what these ministries were in the first century and in the thought of God. I believe that when this happens, many of those people will be led in brand-new directions. And those directions will undoubtedly lead them to break with cherished traditions and popular concepts. Yet only by these elements will the house of God begin to be restored on a broad scale.

As the builder of the *ekklesia*, the Lord Jesus Christ desires nothing less.

CHAPTER 6

HEAD OF THE CHURCH

He is the head of the body, the church: who is the
beginning, the firstborn from the dead; that in
all things he might have the preeminence.

Colossians 1:18 KJV

Throughout the New Testament, there is a subtle distinction between the headship of Christ and the lordship of Jesus.

The *headship* of Christ virtually always has in view Christ's relationship with His body (Eph. 1:22–23; 4:15; 5:23; Col. 1:18; 2:19). The *lordship* of Christ virtually always has in view His relationship with His individual disciples (Matt. 7:21–22; Luke 6:46; Acts 16:31; Rom. 10:9, 13; 1 Cor. 6:17).

What lordship is to the *individual*, headship is to the *church*. Headship and lordship are two dimensions of the same thing. Headship is lordship worked out in the corporate life of God's people.

A believer may truly submit to the lordship of Jesus in his or her personal life. He may obey what he understands in the Bible. She may pray fervently. He may live self-sacrificially. Yet at the same time, these people may know nothing about shared ministry, mutual submission, or corporate testimony. To be subject to the headship of Jesus is to respond to His will regarding the life and practice of the church. Submission to the headship of Christ includes obtaining God's mind through mutual ministry and sharing, obeying the Holy Spirit through mutual subjection and servanthood, and testifying to Jesus Christ collectively through mutual sharing and corporate witness.

Submission to the headship of Christ incarnates the New Testament reality that Jesus is not only Lord of the *lives of women and men*; He is also Master of the *life of the church*. One of the examples in which this became strongly apparent to me was through the life of a young brother in Christ who visited one of our open-participatory church meetings. The young man was saved before he visited us. And from what I could tell, he had a strong devotional life. But he would show up once in a while for our meetings, and when he did show up, he was quiet through most of them.

He continued to visit our gatherings on and off for several months. Then he moved away to another city to attend college there.

Several months later, he returned. Through a series of poor choices, frustrating events, and personal convictions, he had ended his academic career. With a broken voice, he communicated that more than anything he simply missed being a part of the church. I found this interesting, as he wasn't exactly devoted to the group when he was in town, and he never really participated or functioned much.

The next week, however, he threw himself into the life of the church. If there was a practical need, he was helping with it. If there was an opportunity to pursue Christ with others, he showed up. If there was a decision-making meeting, he was there and he participated. He even started to function in our open meetings, and his contributions were edifying. Then slowly, we began to see his friends coming to the meetings. His friends were inspired by his story of redemption, faith, and community. And they were drawn to "come and see."

This young man's life was changed forever when he simply saw a group of people responding to a Jesus he didn't know too well. He was seeing Jesus in corporate expression. But it took his going to college, having a bad experience there, and coming back again to realize he needed Christ and His body. He was awakened to the fact that he needed face-to-face community.

This little story is so familiar and common that it can be multiplied by many who have been part of churches that are strong on intense community and mutual sharing. The young man's story is an example of what it means to make Christ head over one's life.

Interestingly, Paul said that when Christ's headship is established in His body, He will become head over all things in the universe (Col. 1:16–18).

Five Aspects of Christ's Headship Today

1. As the Head, Jesus Seeks to Express His Character and Nature through His Body

The purpose of a physical body is to express the life that's in it. It's the same with the body of Christ. It exists so that Jesus can express His personality in a visible way.

The local body of Christ is called to gather together regularly to display God's life through the ministry of every believer. How?

One of the normative ways in the New Testament was through open-participatory meetings where every member of the believing priesthood functioned, ministered, and expressed the living God (1 Cor. 14:26; 1 Pet. 2:5; Heb. 10:24–25).

God dwells in every Christian and can inspire any of us

to share with the church something that comes from Him. In the first century, every Christian had both the right and the privilege of speaking to the community. This is the practical expression of the New Testament doctrine of the priesthood of all believers.

The purpose of the open-participatory gathering is to edify the entire church and to display, express, and reveal the Lord through the members of the body to principalities and powers in heavenly places (Eph. 3:8–11).

The Greek word for church that I've been using throughout this book, *ekklesia*, literally means "assembly." This meshes nicely with the dominant thought in Paul's letters that the church is Christ in corporate expression (1 Cor. 12:1–27; Eph. 1:22–23; 4:1–16).

From a human perspective, the purpose of the church meeting is mutual edification. But from God's perspective, the purpose of the gathering is to express His glorious Son and make Him visible.

Put another way, we gather together so that the Lord Jesus can manifest Himself in His fullness. When that happens, the body is edified. Note that the only way that Christ can be properly expressed is if *every* member of a church freely supplies the aspect of the Lord that he or she has received. The Lord Jesus cannot be fully disclosed through only one member. He is far too rich for that (Eph. 3:8).

So if the hand doesn't function in the gathering, Christ will not be manifested in fullness. Likewise, if the eyes fail to function, the Lord will be limited in His self-revelation.

On the other hand, when every member of a local assembly functions in the meeting, Christ is seen. He is made visible because He is *assembled* in our midst.

Consider the analogy of a puzzle. When each puzzle piece is properly positioned in relation to the other pieces, the puzzle is assembled. The net effect? We see the entire picture. It's the same way with Christ and His church.

2. As the Head, Jesus Continues His Earthly Ministry

Luke began the book of Acts with this remark:

> The first account I composed, Theophilus,
> about all that Jesus *began* to do and teach,
> until the day when He was taken up to heaven.
> (1:1–2)

Notice the word *began*. The "first account" Luke was referring to is the gospel of Luke. The implication of this sentence is that Luke's new volume, Acts, is a record of what Jesus *continued* to do and teach from His ascension onward.

Consequently, the theme of Acts is Christ's continuing presence, already found in the name *Emmanuel* ("God with us"), as a present reality.

No longer visibly present to the human eye, Jesus is still at work in His people by the Spirit. The story of Acts is the story of Christ's work on earth through His servants as they are energized and directed by the Spirit of Christ.

When Jesus Christ ascended into heaven, He chose to express Himself through a body of believers to continue His life and ministry on earth. That ministry is spelled out in Luke 4:18–19 (NIV):

> The Spirit of the Lord is on me,
>> because he has anointed me
>> to proclaim good news to the poor.
> He has sent me to proclaim freedom for the
>> prisoners
>> and recovery of sight for the blind,
> to set the oppressed free,
>> to proclaim the year of the Lord's favor.

We meet it again in Acts 10:38 (NIV): "God anointed Jesus of Nazareth with the Holy Spirit and power, and ... he went around doing good and healing all who were under the power of the devil, because God was with him."

Throughout His ministry, Jesus showed what the kingdom of God was all about by loving outcasts, befriending the
oppressed, healing the sick, cleansing the lepers, caring for the
poor, driving out demons, forgiving sins, and so forth. If you
peel back His miracles, the common denominator underneath
them all is that He was alleviating human suffering and showing what the future kingdom of God looks like.

When Jesus did His miracles, He was indicating that He
was reversing the effects of the curse.

In Jesus' ministry, a bit of the future had penetrated the
present. Jesus embodied the future kingdom of God, where
human suffering will be eradicated, and there will be peace,
justice, freedom, and joy.

The church, which is His body in the world, carries on
this ministry. It stands on the earth as a sign of the coming
kingdom.

The church lives and acts in the reality that Jesus Christ
is the Lord of the world today. It lives in the presence of the
future—in the already-but-not-yet of the kingdom of God.

For this reason, the church is commissioned to proclaim
and embody the kingdom now—to bring a bit of the new creation into the old creation, to bring a piece of heaven into the
earth—demonstrating to the world what it will look like when
God is calling the shots. In the life of the church, God's future
has already begun.

This dimension of the church's mission has to do with how she displays the Christ who indwells her to those outside of her. It has to do with how she expresses Christ to the world.

Jesus fulfilled the mission of Israel in His earthly ministry (Gen. 18:18). But since His resurrection, He has commissioned the church to continue that mission.

Hence, the church exists to fulfill Israel's original calling to be a blessing to all the nations (Gen. 22:18), to bring good news (the gospel) to the poor (Isa. 52:7), and to be a light to the world (49:6).

The church stands in the earth as the new Israel (Gal. 6:16). And she shows forth that the Jesus who walked this earth is the same Christ who has taken up residence within her members.

3. As the Head, Jesus Directs Both the Church and the Work

Jesus is the Commander-in-Chief of His church and His work. Following are some examples of how Jesus directs both His church and His work by His Spirit as the head of each:

- The Spirit of Jesus led Philip to join a chariot where a man was reading Scripture (Acts 8:29).
- Jesus appeared to Paul and called him into apostolic ministry (Acts 9:1–10).

- Jesus appeared to Ananias in a vision and instructed him to help Paul (Acts 9:11–16).

- The Spirit of Jesus spoke to Peter about three men who were looking for him (Acts 10:19).

- The Spirit of Jesus told Peter to go see Cornelius in Caesarea (Acts 11:12).

- The Spirit of Jesus showed Agabus the prophet that there would be a great drought coming to the world (Acts 11:28).

- The Spirit of Jesus instructed some men who were praying in Antioch to set apart Barnabas and Paul for the work (Acts 13:2).

- The Spirit of Jesus forbade Paul to preach the gospel in Asia (Acts 16:6).

- Jesus gave Paul a dream, directing him and his team to go into Macedonia (Acts 16:9–10).

- Jesus appeared to Paul in a vision and told him to speak boldly in the city of Corinth (Acts 18:9–10).

- The Spirit of Jesus witnessed to Paul in every city that he would be in chains and suffer afflictions (Acts 20:23).

- The Spirit of Jesus spoke through Agabus

the prophet about Paul's future in Jerusalem (Acts 21:10–11).

- Jesus appeared to Paul while he was praying in the temple in Jerusalem and told him to leave the city (Acts 22:18–21).

- Jesus stood by Paul when he was on trial, encouraged him, and told him what was to come (Acts 23:11).

- Jesus said to Paul, "My grace is sufficient for you, for [my] power is perfected in weakness" (2 Cor. 12:9).

- Paul received direction, reassurance, and encouragement from Jesus (2 Tim. 4:16–17).

- The Spirit of Jesus called and sent out workers (Acts 13:1–3; Gal. 1:1; 1 Cor. 1:17; 12:7–11; Eph. 4:7–16; 1 Tim. 1:12).

- Jesus worked with the members of His church, confirming their message with signs (Mark 16:20).

In the book of Acts, we find the phrase "get up and go" repeated several times. Jesus said it to Ananias in Acts 9:11. He said it to Peter again in Acts 10:20. Ananias went, and so did Peter. As head of the church, Jesus still says, "Get up and go," to His disciples today.

4. As the Head, Jesus Nourishes His Body

The way we feed our bodies is through our mouths. Jesus does the same with His body, of which we are a part.

Christ, then, is our Caretaker. He nourishes and cherishes His body:

> No one ever hated his own flesh, but nourishes and cherishes it, just as Christ also does the church. (Eph. 5:29)

Christ the head feeds His body through the ministry and functioning of each of its members (Eph. 4:16). For this reason, it's important to be dependent on the body of Christ, allowing "every joint" to supply its portion to us.

In like manner, it's critical that we function also, feeding the other sheep in the Lord's fold.

5. As the Head, Jesus Is the Source of the Church's Life

Jesus supplies all that His body needs, and we derive our life and being from Him.

"Christ ... is our life," as Colossians put it (3:4).

The head in heaven dispenses His life through His Spirit, who empowers the members of His body on earth.

The Jesus of the Gospels may appear remote and unavailable, but He lives inside every believer by faith and is as close to us as is the breath of our mouths.

> No longer I ... but Christ lives in me. (Gal. 2:20)

> What Christ has accomplished through me. (Rom. 15:18)

> I can do all things through [Christ] who strengthens me. (Phil. 4:13)

As followers of Jesus and children of God, we can live by His indwelling life. Jesus was "crucified in weakness" but now "lives by the power of God" (2 Cor. 13:3–4 ESV). He does this within His people.

The Eternal Purpose

The eternal purpose of God is centered upon making Jesus the absolute head over all things. God's goal is the establishment of the complete sovereignty and supremacy of His Son.

His driving passion is to make His Son preeminent over everything. All of God's activities are toward this end. Hence, the chief work of the Holy Spirit in this age is to establish the headship of Christ in His body, to the uttermost.

Accordingly, the Holy Spirit will break down and devastate everything that opposes, obstructs, and hinders the Lord's sovereign rule in the hearts of His people. He will stand against all that gets in the way of God's ultimate intention of establishing the centrality and supremacy of His Son over all things. Strikingly, before Christ can be made preeminent over all things, He must first have the preeminence among His own people. Colossians 1:18 puts it this way:

He is the head of the body, the church … that
in all things he might have the preeminence.
(KJV; see also Eph. 5:23)

The great need today in the body of Christ is to reinstate the headship of Christ. Tragically, all sorts of things have replaced Christ's headship. Church boards, committee meetings, church leaders, church programs, man-made rules and regulations, and so on, have often supplanted the headship of Jesus Christ.

Whenever there is a decision before us regarding the Lord's work or the Lord's people, the salient question should not be, "What do we think should be done?" or "What can we agree upon as spiritual leaders?" Rather it should be, *"What does the Lord want in this situation?"*

With respect to the church, when two people make a decision independent of the head, it constitutes conspiracy.

Christ alone has the right to rule His church—not any human or committee. It is His body, not ours. We all belong to Him. He has purchased us with a costly price, and thus He alone possesses full rights over us.

When Christ has His full and rightful place as head and absolute Lord over His people, then so many problems are resolved.

Consider the profound problems that the church in Corinth faced—carnality, divisions, envy, self-absorption, blasphemy, pride, immorality, strife, civil discord, and rivalry. Chapters 1–11 of 1 Corinthians paint a pitiful picture of the corruption in that assembly. What a tremendous burden for Paul—the man who planted and cared for that church. But what was his answer to it all? What was the all-inclusive solution that he shared in 1 Corinthians? It was simply this:

> I determined not to know any thing among
> you, save Jesus Christ, and him crucified....
> For other foundation can no man lay than that
> is laid, which is Jesus Christ. (2:2; 3:11 KJV)

The answer was quite plain: that Jesus Christ be given His rightful place in the church. Can you see the force of that?

When God's people get ahold of the greatness of their Lord and put Him in His rightful place, all of their troubles are dealt with. When Christ is presented in power and life, our problems get resolved.

God's aim in this hour is for us to make Christ's headship a practical reality in our lives and in our churches.

Such a way, however, is costly. It is a hard thing to yield our rights to the Lord, to wait on the Lord, and to put the absolute rule, authority, and decision-making rights into the hands of the Holy Spirit.

It tests whether we are going to put our hands on things or yield all rights to Christ. We must understand, however, that if Jesus Christ will return to reign on this earth in His fullness, His people must first give Him the preeminence in their midst.

In God's plan, all things begin with the church. James told us that we are the "firstfruits of all he created" (1:18 NIV). That includes this business of Him reigning over all things.

Holding Fast to the Head

Make no mistake about it. Holding fast to the headship of Christ (as Paul put it in Colossians) is not something that we are to practice as a last resort. Too often the mentality among Christians is, "I will do whatever *I can*, using my own cleverness, gifts, and abilities, and only rely upon the Lord when

I cannot do any more." This is foolish thinking at best. Our human ideas and philosophies cannot fulfill one fragment of God's work.

A great deal of our ecclesiastical traditions and programs are nothing more than wood, hay, and stubble. The church is a spiritual organism. Only that which comes out of God's indwelling life can accomplish His purpose.

Under the old covenant, Moses commanded that no oil be "poured on man's flesh" (Exod. 30:32 NKJV). So, too, the Spirit of God cannot anoint that which comes out of our human fleshly ideas. Recall the words of the Lord Jesus: "Without Me you can do nothing" (John 15:5 NKJV).

All of this will meet nodding heads from most Christians. But is it a reality? Is Jesus Christ truly the head of your church, or is someone else? Does the structure of your church allow for Jesus Christ to lead and direct His people through His body, or does it prevent that from happening? And how about your life?

God desires to sum up all things in His Son. That which originates from fallen humanity's ideas, traditions, and systems will not last. Only that which comes out of Christ can find God's highest blessing.

Even now, the Lord is awaiting a people to give Him that place of preeminence. When God's people put themselves under His direct headship, the result is unity (Ps. 133). One day

Christ will indeed be the "head over *all things* to the church" (Eph. 1:22 ESV), nothing excluded. His present-day ministry as head of the church is moving the world in that direction.

CHAPTER 7

LORD OF THE WORLD

*Therefore let all the house of Israel know for
certain that God has made Him both Lord and
Christ—this Jesus whom you crucified.*

Acts 2:36

We've seen that the present-day ministry of Jesus Christ is multi-faceted. Jesus hasn't retired since He ascended into heaven. He's not gone on vacation. Instead, He's active in the world. And He's active in our lives.

The lordship of Jesus over the entire world went into effect when God the Father raised Christ from the dead and enthroned Him in heaven. At that moment, Jesus of Nazareth became this world's true Lord—Lord of heaven and earth, possessing all authority.

All authority has been given to Me in heaven
and on earth. (Matt. 28:18)

However, Jesus will someday return to this earth and take
His rightful place as King of the world, putting all enemies
under His feet. When this occurs, everyone will acknowledge
His absolute lordship:

> For this reason also, God highly exalted Him,
> and bestowed on Him the name which is above
> every name, so that at the name of Jesus every
> knee will bow, of those who are in heaven and
> on earth and under the earth, and that every
> tongue will confess that Jesus Christ is Lord,
> to the glory of God the Father. (Phil. 2:9–11)

> Therefore repent and return, so that your
> sins may be wiped away, in order that times
> of refreshing may come from the presence of
> the Lord; and that He may send Jesus, the
> Christ appointed for you, whom heaven must
> receive until the period of restoration of all
> things about which God spoke by the mouth
> of His holy prophets from ancient time. (Acts
> 3:19–21; see also Acts 2:32–36)

Three Gospels

"The world," Martin Luther said, "is like a drunken peasant. If you lift him into the saddle on one side, he will fall again on the other side." The same can be said about the Christian life.

In the first century, there were three gospels. And those three gospels are still with us today.

Legalism

Some contemporary Christians have accepted the gospel of legalism. Believers in the Reformed tradition tend to restrict legalism as the attempt to earn salvation by human works. But for the genuine Christian who is saved by grace, legalism goes much deeper than that. Legalists are people who believe that salvation is by grace alone but that sanctification comes by their own efforts of trying hard to be "good Christians." Legalists tend to push their own personal standards onto everyone else. They are quick to judge other people's motives, thinking the worst of them and their intentions. They confuse obedience with trying to serve God in their own strength. They demand that other people do things they themselves would never carry out. They regard the sins of others as more severe and grievous than their own. (Philip Yancey described the legalist perfectly when he said, "Christians get very angry toward other Christians who sin differently than they do.")

Legalists also feel that it's their right to become intrusive meddlers, or as Peter put it incisively, "Busybod[ies] in other people's matters" (1 Pet. 4:15 NKJV). They are blind to their own self-righteousness, and they pride themselves on being "clean" on the outside (without realizing that they are defiled on the inside). For all of these reasons, they unwittingly bring a lot of pain and heartache into the lives of others; yet sadly they seem to be out of touch with this.

When I was in my teens, I came to the Lord through a legalistic denomination. I was fed a steady diet of the gospel of legalism and was surrounded by legalists. Thus I used to be a legalist without realizing it. But God was merciful.

Libertinism

In reaction to legalism and the devastation it brings to other people, some have accepted the gospel of libertinism. Libertines are folks who live the way they want and have skirted the lordship of Christ and all that it means. They are apt to justify carnality by pulling the "grace card," the "I'm free in Christ" card, and the "Don't judge me" card. For libertines, grace becomes a license to live in the flesh and silence their consciences (see Jude v. 4).

Some libertines have rationalized that they can continue to practice a particular transgression because God is "cool with that," regardless of the carnage it brings. However, a mark of sin is that it produces unnecessary pain in the lives of others. Sin and love are the exact opposites. Love is benefiting others at the expense of yourself. Sin is benefiting yourself at the expense of others. Sin is selfishness; love is selflessness. Love is a greater force than sin—God's life is more powerful than Satan's nature, and "love covers a multitude of sins" (1 Pet. 4:8).

Some libertines have gone so far into deception that they have reinvented Jesus in their own image to justify their rebellion against the Lord and clothe it with spiritual talk. Others have gone further off the beam and have become practical atheists.

Note that there are degrees of legalism and degrees of libertinism. But these descriptions should give the general flavor of each.

In short, the libertine lives as if there is no God. The legalist lives as though she or he is God to everyone else.

Both attitudes are incompatible with the life of Christ.

Lordship and Liberty

What complicates the situation further is that the legalist doesn't know that he or she is a legalist and tends to view all nonlegalists as libertines. And the libertine doesn't know that she or he is a libertine and tends to view all nonlibertines as legalists.

Without the Holy Spirit's illumination, this deception is difficult if not impossible to break. The truth is, we have *all* sinned and "fall short of the glory of God" (Rom. 3:23). And we all need Jesus Christ to forgive, deliver, and keep us each day from both the defiling acts of the flesh *and* the self-righteousness of the flesh.

In contrast to the gospel of legalism and libertinism is the gospel of Jesus and Paul, which I call the gospel of lordship and liberty.

Jesus is Savior and Lord. Submitting to Christ's lordship sets one free from the bondage of the self-righteousness of the flesh on the one hand, and the works of the flesh on the other.

Legalism is the counterfeit of the lordship of Christ, and libertinism is the counterfeit of the liberty of the Spirit.

But the truth is, submission to Christ's lordship is the gateway to the liberty of the Spirit.

The gospel of the New Testament is rooted in reality—the real Jesus—and it sets us free from the defilement of the flesh *and* the self-righteousness of the flesh, both of which come off the same tree. Both bring bondage and cause untold pain to others, for both violate love, the nature of God's own life.

One of the things I've learned in my spiritual journey is that the closer someone gets to Jesus Christ, the less judgmental, self-righteous, harsh toward others, and selfish he or she will be.

Those who are under the lordship of Christ possess the liberty to genuinely love others (Gal. 5:1–6).

The Central Issue of the Universe

According to Matthew 12:24–28, two kingdoms are at war with each other: the kingdom of God and the kingdom of Satan—the kingdom of light and the kingdom of darkness.

Behind what you and I see, there is a furious battle raging in the spiritual world. Behind everything that goes on in this world, there is a sinister force. And that force involves us.

In this battle, there are no civilians. But there are many casualties. No one is neutral.

Jesus plainly said, "He who is not with Me is against Me" (Luke 11:23).

If you are not with Jesus Christ, you are with His Enemy. You are helping to advance either His kingdom or the other one.

Both of these kingdoms are seeking one thing: *worship*.

The central question of the universe is about who will have the worship. It's about who will have the authority. It's over who will sit on the throne and be in charge.

This is the issue that lies behind all that is taking place on the earth today.

When the Conflict Began

Let's hit rewind and see where this cosmic conflict began. Christians have traditionally understood Isaiah 14 and Ezekiel 28 to have a dual meaning. One of the meanings is that there was a rebellion in heavenly places. The following was said about Lucifer, one of God's angels:

> How you have fallen from heaven,
> O star of the morning, son of the dawn!
> You have been cut down to the earth,
> You who have weakened the nations!
> But you said in your heart,
> "I will ascend to heaven;
> I will raise my throne above the stars of God,
> And I will sit on the mount of assembly
> In the recesses of the north.
> I will ascend above the heights of the clouds;
> I will make myself like the Most High." (Isa. 14:12–14)

Self-ambition, self-assertiveness, self-absorption, and pride filled the heart of this angel. Lucifer fell and took other angelic beings with him.

Here are some of the names of our Enemy according to Scripture, all of which give us insight into his character:

- Slanderer, the meaning of *devil* (Matt. 4:1)
- The accuser of the brethren (Rev. 12:10)
- The Evil One (1 John 5:19)
- The tempter (1 Thess. 3:5; James 1:13)
- The "ruler of this world" (John 12:31)
- A roaring lion (1 Pet. 5:8)
- A thief and a robber (John 10:10)
- A murderer, a liar, and the "father of lies" (John 8:44)

According to Genesis 1:26–28, God created humans to do two things:

1. To express God's image
2. To rule and subdue the earth

When Adam and Eve fell, disobeying God, two things occurred:

1. They marred God's image. Humans became something other than what God created them to be.
2. They lost God's authority over the earth. The Devil seized Adam and Eve's authority and he (the Devil) became the ruler of the earth

in this present age. As a result, God's rule on
earth was thwarted.

Put another way, Adam committed high treason against God.
And in so doing, he handed the earth over to Satan's control. This
is why the New Testament calls Satan "the god of this world," "the
ruler of this world," "the evil one," and "the prince of the power
of the air" (2 Cor. 4:3–4; John 12:31; 1 John 5:19; Eph. 2:1–2).

Death entered into the world, along with sickness, disease,
thorns, thistles, natural disasters, and other problems.

From that day forward, the earth—over which humans
once had control—was now in the hands of God's Enemy.

This explains why Satan could tempt Jesus with the offer of
all the kingdoms of the world if Jesus would just worship him
(Luke 4:5–8).

God's Reaction

God, however, did not remain passive. He took action to undo
the consequences of the fallen human race. He had a plan to
get His authority back into the hands of humans.

The Old Testament unveils this plan. Beginning with God's
chosen man, Abraham, the Lord created a nation. And from
that nation came a Man—the One whom the Bible calls "the
last Adam" and "the second man" (1 Cor. 15:45, 47).

The purpose of the second Adam was to recover what the first Adam had lost in the fall and to destroy what Satan had gained.

It was through this Man, Jesus Christ, that the kingdom of God found expression. It was through Christ's death, resurrection, and ascension that God's kingdom began to invade the present kingdom.

The ultimate defeat of Satan's kingdom was accomplished through Christ's death on the cross.

Christ's work on the cross is God's answer to the central question of the universe. It went straight to the root of the problem—defeating the Evil One and undoing his consequences.

Through Christ's death and resurrection, God reversed the effects of the fall in two ways:

1. What the Devil gained in the fall, Christ reclaimed at the cross.
2. Through Christ's death, Satan's whole legal standing was destroyed. His rights over the earth and over human souls were annihilated.

Through His death, Christ terminated the entire old creation. Through His resurrection, He became the head of a new creation.

So what humans lost in the fall, Christ recovered through His death and resurrection.

Consequently, all who receive Christ and come under His lordship are free from the Enemy's power.

Our Present Warfare

So if Jesus won the victory over God's Enemy, why do we see Satan operating in the world today two millennia later? Why do we see the effects of sin, death, and the curse all around us ... *still?*

The answer: Jesus stripped God's Enemy of the power and authority he gained through humanity's fall. But God is now waiting for His people to work with Him and put into effect the finished, victorious, and triumphant work of Christ.

God has finished His work. But He has called His people to complete what Jesus began and to bring Jesus into what is rightfully His—to restore the earth to God's complete and perfect rule by the power of the Holy Spirit until the Lord returns to finish the job.

Spiritual V-Day

Again, the right hand is the place of honor, dominion, power, and glory. In the Bible, sitting on the right hand denotes supremacy—whether at a table of patriarchs or over the universe.

So Jesus is now the Lord of heaven and earth. He's in charge. He calls the shots.

But turn on the news and ask yourself, Does it appear that Jesus is ruling the world?

Oscar Cullmann gave the superb illustration of a great war. In a great war, there's often one battle that decides the war's outcome.[1] After this one battle is won, it's clear to all who the victor is. However, it's impossible to tell how long the war will keep going on after this victory is secured.

D-day is the day the battle was won and victory declared. V-day is the victory celebration that lies in the future.

The battle between good and evil was won by Jesus at Calvary. When Christ died and rose again, He declared victory over the hostile forces of the demonic world.

The most powerful of these forces is death itself.

However, even though Jesus conquered death in His resurrection, death is still active. But for those who are in Christ, death has lost its sting. Believers don't need to fear death. In fact, believers don't "die"; they "sleep," according to the New Testament. They don't taste true death.

In the future, however, Jesus will return again and deal death its final blow. V-day will arrive.

For this reason, 2 Timothy 1:10 says that death has already been abolished, while 1 Corinthians 15:26 says that death will finally be abolished when Christ returns.

---

1   Oscar Cullmann, *Christ and Time* (Philadelphia: Westminster Press, 1964).

The hostile forces that Jesus conquered at the cross are now "weak and beggarly elements" (Gal. 4:9 KJV) that do not have dominion over God's people.

Jesus has conquered Satan and vanquished death, but these defeated foes aren't yet silenced. The Son is at the Father's right hand, but He's not sedentary. He hasn't gone on vacation. He's busily engaged in working through His body and overcoming His Enemy. The King and His subjects are united in victory and authority.

Consequently, Jesus still poses a threat to this world's rulers. He's not dissolved into heavenly realms. He's alive and active, working through our hands and feet.

The Man who once walked among us sits on God's throne. And He's not detached from the affairs of His creation below.

The Lord's Instrument

The Lord's instrument for complete victory over the world is a company of people who have come under Christ's rule and possess His life and authority. They—the body of Jesus Christ—are the tool that God uses to crush Satan's head practically and visibly.

The *ekklesia* fills the gap between the ascension and the second coming.

Where is Jesus now? He's reigning at the right hand of God

the Father until the day He returns to planet Earth in glory. Christ is "at the right hand of God, having gone into heaven, after angels and authorities and powers had been subjected to Him" (1 Pet. 3:22).

For this reason, Scripture calls Him "the ruler of the kings of the earth" (Rev. 1:5) and the head over all rule and authority (Col. 2:10).

But as the body of Christ wages warfare against God's Enemy, exercising the reality of D-day, Jesus will finally return, and His kingdom of God will fill the whole earth "as the waters cover the sea." V-day will be here.

> For the earth will be filled with the knowledge
> of the glory of the LORD,
> as the waters cover the sea. (Hab. 2:14 NIV)

> Then comes the end, when He [Jesus] hands
> over the kingdom to the God and Father, when
> He has abolished all rule and all authority and
> power. For He must reign until He has put all
> His enemies under His feet. The last enemy that
> will be abolished is death. (1 Cor. 15:24–26)

Even though he is a defeated foe, Satan repudiates the right of God to take his throne. And he is still seeking to take over all things.

But Jesus has already destroyed his power. God's Enemy, then, is now an illegal alien roaming the earth.

One of Satan's royal tactics is to convince humans that he doesn't exist and to keep them ignorant of their true condition. Satan's basic nature is selfishness. He is a liar, a thief, a killer, and a devourer. And his main tool is deception (John 8:44; 10:10; 1 Pet. 5:8).

By contrast, God is looking for His people to come into His kingdom and stand on this earth for His rights, making Him absolute Lord and doing warfare with His Enemy:

> Then the seventh angel sounded; and there were loud voices in heaven, saying, "The kingdom of the world has become the kingdom of our Lord and of His Christ; and He will reign forever and ever." (Rev. 11:15)

The central question of the universe must be answered by us all, and it is this: Who will have *your* worship? Who will have *your* life? Who will have *your* allegiance?

Instead of Christians waiting for the Lord to return, God is waiting for the church to step into its role of taking the authority of Jesus and doing damage to Satan's kingdom. Not by political or human energy and power, but by the power of the Holy Spirit.

Separating What God Has Joined

I want to address a somewhat popular cliché that I believe misses the mark on what the New Testament teaches concerning the kingdom of God. Here's the cliché:

> Jesus mentioned the church only twice, but He mentioned the kingdom over a hundred times. So He really doesn't care about the church as much as He does the kingdom.

Have you heard it before? Maybe even passed it on?

Allow me to take dead aim at this line of thought. It's specious reasoning at best.

Behold, I show you a mystery: Without the church, there is no kingdom. And without the kingdom, there is no church.

Jesus Christ incarnates the kingdom, and He is inseparable from His body.

When the church is functioning properly in a given place, she is the manifestation of God's ruling presence. She reveals Christ; that is, she expresses the kingdom—the righteousness, peace, and joy in the Holy Spirit.

She shows forth the rule of God, makes visible the reign of God and the justice, freedom, and peace that go with it.

To separate the kingdom from the church is like separating light from visibility.

Having said that, I believe the "Jesus only mentioned the church twice and the kingdom over a hundred times" argument is based on a superficial analysis of the Gospels that is grossly misleading.

This line of reasoning is not dissimilar to those who say, "The Trinity is *never* mentioned in the Bible; therefore, to say that Father, Son, and Spirit are three yet one is false."

The term *Godhead* is used only three times in the New Testament. Does that then mean that the Godhead is not mentioned or referred to in the New Testament? Or that it's not important?

Hardly.

In like manner, John 14, 15, 16, and 17 are dripping full of the Godhead. So is most of the gospel of John. Though *Godhead* isn't mentioned once in John's gospel. And neither is the word *Trinity*. Yet the Godhead is present all throughout the book of John in living color.

The Church in Fresh Perspective

With that thought in mind, let me make a radical statement:

The Lord Jesus Christ mentioned and referred to the church more than He did the kingdom of God.

But He didn't do it by using the word *ekklesia*.

Remember that small band of disciples Jesus called to Himself and lived with for three and a half years?

They were the Twelve, added to what Luke called "the women." Probably around twenty individuals in all.

Those twenty people were a community that lived a shared life under the headship of Jesus Christ. Christ was the center of their lives and fellowship.

In other words: *They were the embryonic expression of the* ekklesia.

What is *ekklesia* (church) in the New Testament? It's a community of believers who share a common life in Christ, assemble together regularly, and make Jesus central, supreme, and head over their lives together.

Those twenty believers were the community of the King. And that's precisely what the *ekklesia* is.

Each local *ekklesia* is an outpost of the kingdom of God. Put another way, each community of believers that enthrones Jesus as Lord is a colony of God's kingdom in a sinful world.

Consequently, every time you see the Twelve (and the women) with Jesus in the Gospels, you're seeing a microcosm of the *ekklesia*.

And virtually every time Jesus spoke to His disciples and used the word *you* ...

You are the light of the world (Matt. 5:14).

You are the salt of the earth (Matt 5:13).

The Helper ... will teach *you* all things (John 14:26 ESV).

I am the vine, *you* are the branches. (John 15:5).

... He was referring to the church.

In addition, when John used the word *we*, he was most often speaking of the church: "For from his fullness *we* have all received, grace upon grace" (John 1:16 ESV).

Do you remember when Jesus said, "Unless a grain of wheat falls into the ground and dies, it remains alone. But if it dies, it produces a lot of grain" (John 12:24 ISV)? The phrase "a lot of grain" refers to the church.

How about when Jesus referred to His brethren? "Go to my brethren, and say unto them, I ascend unto my Father" (John 20:17 KJV).

Or how about when He prayed for His disciples in John 17 and said, "I do not ask on behalf of these alone, but for those also who will believe in Me through their word" (v. 20)?

Who are the "those who will believe in Me"?

The church.

Who are the Lord's "brethren"?

The church.

There are eighty-five unique references to the kingdom in the Synoptic Gospels. And five in the gospel of John. So the Gospels total ninety unique references to the kingdom.

Put that against the many references to the church given earlier, and the count is less for the kingdom.

When we come to the New Testament writings (Acts to Revelation), the kingdom is mentioned 31 times and the church is found 77 times.

The word *brethren*—which refers to the brothers and sisters in the churches—is used 249 times in Acts through Revelation.

The word *saints* (holy ones), which is a reference to the individual believers in the churches, is used 60 times.

Now, in light of all of the above, can we please stop pitting the church against the kingdom?

To do such is to violate the gospel and the whole drift of New Testament revelation.

Accordingly, you cannot separate the Lord Jesus Christ from the kingdom of God, and you cannot separate the church of Jesus Christ from the kingdom. What God has joined together, let no one put asunder.

In short, Jesus is this earth's true Lord, and the church is His instrument for making this fact a visible reality.

CHAPTER 8

JESUS CHRIST TODAY

Jesus Christ is the same yesterday and today and forever.

Hebrews 13:8 NIV

So who is Jesus today?

Is He someone we remember and try to emulate? Or is He someone who is living and active and has a specific ministry?

In the previous pages, we've seen that the ascension of Jesus marked the commencement of His present-day ministry.

In reaching His own destiny, Jesus reached it for us, too. Christ led us to the place that neither Abraham, Moses, Joshua, nor David could ever lead us.

Jesus presents Himself to God the Father as high priest, as both offerer and offering. Since we are in Christ, as the Father receives Jesus, He also receives you and me.

When Christ ascended into heaven, He did not drop his human body. He is still the human Jesus with a glorified human body. In 1 Corinthians 15, Paul called the glorified body of Jesus a "spiritual body" (v. 44). This doesn't mean that He was a ghost. It means that His renewed physical body was energized by the Holy Spirit after His resurrection. In His glorified body, Jesus could eat and drink physical food. He could also pass through walls (Luke 24:13–35; John 20:26).

Consequently, Jesus continues His incarnation after His ascension and receives our humanity into Himself. He didn't dispose of our humanity but took it with Him into heavenly realms. Jesus penetrated the splendor of heaven wearing our flesh, bringing us to His Father.

Theologically speaking, the ascension reveals that Jesus' incarnation continues, and the Father, Spirit, and Son have taken up our humanity into God's bosom forever.

Jesus retains His humanity and His divinity and reigns over the world as the God-Man until all enemies are put "under His feet" (1 Cor. 15:20–28).

We, the collective people of God, are the continuing incarnation and presence of Jesus on the earth today.

Did Jesus Fail?

To natural minds, Jesus' ministry ended in failure on two counts: (1) a failure in Galilee when most of His followers turned away from Him, and (2) a failure in Jerusalem when His disciples deserted Him, and He was put to death on a cross.

But the work of Christ went on.

Jesus was raised by His Father and ascended to God's right hand (Eph. 1:20–22; Col. 3:1; Heb. 1:3; 7:26; 8:1; 10:12). But He didn't retire, nor was He detached from the world. Instead, He began His present-day ministry, where He became powerfully present with His followers.

His followers weren't to carry on Jesus' work in His absence. No, Jesus shared His ministry with them (Mark 16:19–20; Acts 1:1–2).

The work of God today is still the work of Christ. He carries it out in His enthroned state, withdrawn from visible sight but active in Spirit in and through His followers.

The book of Acts would be more accurately called "The Acts of the Risen Christ through His Apostles."

While Christ is no longer visible to unaided human sight, He is still powerfully active through His disciples. Jesus doesn't operate us by remote control. He's present with us by His Spirit. He's not a clockmaker who sets the work going and then leaves it to go on by its own momentum. No, Jesus keeps it going Himself.

Jesus still *is*—present tense—the visible image of the invisible God (Col. 1:15). When we see Jesus operating through His people, we see God. Jesus is still the human face of God.

True Freedom

As our mediator, Jesus carries our names on His shoulders and breast just as the high priest of the Old Testament carried the names of Israel on his shoulders and breast.

Christ's position of sitting at the right hand of the Father signifies *rest*—it denotes a completed and finished work. There's no more to be done. Jesus' blood was completely and eternally accepted by God the Father.

Jesus' sacrifice on the cross was once and for all, but His ministry of intercession is eternal. He is the Son of God and the Son of Man eternally.

As high priest, Jesus makes intercession on the basis of His own spotless perfection. It's as if He says to the Father, "Receive Me for them. Forgive all of their imperfections on the basis of My sinless perfection."

In the presence of God, the mighty perfection of Jesus is the answer for our sins. Hence, we don't come before God the Father in ourselves. We come to God in Christ, by Christ, and through Christ. And God is satisfied with us in Christ (1 Cor. 1:30).

For this reason, Jesus is the author of our eternal salvation (Heb. 5:9 NKJV).

So when we speak of Jesus interceding for us, Jesus isn't reminding the Father about what He did. (How could the Father forget?) Nor is He pleading His sacrifice before a reluctant God.

Christ's very presence in heaven as the Crucified One constitutes the greatest prayer and intercession. The wounds of Christ are the unceasing prayers of Jesus. By them, He has secured constant and free access to God's throne (Heb. 4:16).

A guilty conscience, a conscience stained by sin, cannot be purified by anything else but the blood of Christ. No other sacrifice for the sins of humankind is necessary. Jesus' death was a once-and-for-all sacrifice (Heb. 9:26).

Jesus has passed into a realm wherein we have access. We don't have to wait to die to enter it: eternal life begins *now*. The veil has been torn, and the way into the holiest opened.

More remarkably, our great high priest, Jesus, leads our worship "in the midst of the *ekklesia*." Through the Spirit, Christ comes into our midst and offers our praise and worship to a welcoming Father. Through the church, Jesus sings to His Father, leading our praises (Heb. 2:12; 8:1–2).

So Jesus is the perfecter not only of our faith but also of our worship.

This relates to our prayer life as well. We enter into the fellowship that the Son has with His Father (1 John 1:1–3;

1 Cor. 1:9). Jesus is not only the object of our prayers, but He's the means. As our high priest, Christ by the Spirit prays in and through us (Rom. 8:26–27).

According to the New Testament, prayer is in Christ, through Christ, and to Christ.

The Mighty Name of Jesus

In the Scriptures, the name of a person represents who that person is. Thus when the early Christians did something "in Jesus' name," they were doing it in the presence and the authority of Jesus.

Therefore, doing or saying something in Jesus' name is like exercising a God-mandated power of attorney.

Jesus' person is united to His name. For this reason, the New Testament uses believing in Jesus and believing in His name synonymously (John 1:12; 2:23; 3:18; 1 John 5:13).

Before Jesus rose again and ascended, He told His disciples that they hadn't asked anything in His name (John 16:24). But He told them that after His ascension, whatever they asked in His name (or His person) would be granted them by the Father (John 16:23; 14:13–15).

The disciples cast out demons and healed the sick in Jesus' name (Mark 16:17–18; Acts 3:1–6, 16; 16:18; James 5:14).

Salvation is found in "no other name under heaven" (Acts 4:12). The name of Jesus stands above every other name, and at

the name of Jesus, "every knee will bow" in all three realms—
heaven, hell, and earth (Phil. 2:9–11).

Strangely Dim

The ascension demonstrates that we are part of another world,
another realm, another kingdom. As Christians, therefore, we
shouldn't identify ourselves with the present age—whether
country, culture, or race. We are part of a new humanity where
Jesus is head. As "partakers of the divine nature" (2 Pet. 1:4),
we have a source of continuing transformation that empowers
us to transcend nationalism, racism, and culture wars—to be
a people of reconciliation who stand in the gap between the
petty conflicts that often rule this present age.

The ascension shows us that the church ought not to be
captive to the partisan spirit of this present world. We are not
home in this old world, which is passing away. Rather, we are
part of the new heavens and the new earth.

The ascension is God's no to the principalities and powers,
and God's yes to His Son. Jesus has triumphed, and there is no
other Lord but Him (Acts 2:36).

Historically, Christians have made three main errors when
it comes to their relationship to the world. Properly understood, the ascension of Jesus corrects each error.

They are …

Problem 1: Withdrawal from the World

Solution: In His ascension, the body of Christ is Jesus acting in and for the world. Christians are light and salt in a dark world. Recall that when Jesus was on earth in His human body, His main task was to see what His Father was doing and join Himself to it.

Today, our main task is to see what Jesus Christ is doing and join ourselves to it. Thus we don't draw away from the world; we enter into it and follow Jesus wherever He is moving there.

Problem 2: Trying to Bring the Kingdom on Earth

Solution: In His ascension, Jesus brings part of His kingdom on earth now through His *ekklesia*, but He will bring it in its fullness only at His second coming. The kingdom is here already but also not yet. We cannot bring the kingdom into being in our own power. And we cannot bring the kingdom ahead of the King.

Problem 3: Conformity to the World

Solution: In His ascension, Christ lives in His people by the power of His indwelling life. That life keeps us distinct from the world and its values as we answer a higher, more compassionate call. The Lord's ascension also proves that Jesus is Lord. As such, His followers are part of a different kingdom with a different core trajectory.

Looking at all three problems and their solutions, we encounter a paradox in Scripture. And that paradox can be put this way: *for God so loved the world* versus *love not the world*. [1]

We live on earth with the life of eternity in our spirits. The *ekklesia* is a colony of heaven on earth (Eph. 2:18–22; Phil. 3:20–21; 1 Pet. 2:9–12; Heb. 11:13–16).

The Holy Spirit is the reality of Christ's presence and dispenses to us the very life that Jesus lived.

At Pentecost, the Holy Spirit came as the Spirit of the glorified Jesus, the Spirit of the incarnate, crucified, and exalted Christ. The Spirit came to take the life that had interwoven humanity and divinity in the person of Jesus and dispense it to God's people. And He, Christ, promised to be present with us until the consummation of the age (Matt. 28:20).

Knowing that Jesus is ascended and enthroned in heaven, we have assurance of final victory. If we take the time to pay attention and rest in these promises, this knowledge delivers us from fear, depression, and insecurity during the trials and tests of life.

---

1   For details, you can freely listen to my conference message "For God So Loved the World vs. Love Not the World" at http://frankviola.org/lovenottheworld.

Whatever happens, Christ is *still* on the throne and in control. The Jesus of yesterday is the Jesus of today and will one day become the Jesus of tomorrow.

Our representative Man has reached the goal; the forerunner blazes the path for us all.

We are partners of the heavenly calling (Heb. 3:1), pioneers of the heavenly way.

He has dominion over heaven and earth.

He secured the eternal purpose of God and "ascended on high" to bring forth "many sons to glory" (Heb. 2:10; Eph. 4:8). And for reasons hidden in His infinite love and mercy, God has allowed us to participate in Christ's present-day ministry of sanctification and redemption.

We can lay hold of these realities only with the eyes of faith.

I'll close with a statement from a friend of mine named Barbey Meyers. In 2004, I delivered a series of messages on the present-day ministry of Jesus Christ to a local fellowship in Southern California. Barbey was one of the members of this fellowship, and after I traveled back home, she began emailing me the group's reflections on the messages I had delivered while there. Here's a statement from Barbey that was part of those emails:

> In Jesus, the Son of Man, all of the Godhead
> was contained in a single physical body. The

cross broke Jesus open, and through the opening, God's life was subject to reproduction into
prepared vessels in which His role as high priest
would be expressed to the world. Jesus took to
His Father the experience as the Son of Man
and left that experience in His Spirit to be part
of the life He impregnated into those called
to be sons and daughters of God. I'm a needy
human being, but my weaknesses do not plague
me like they used to. They're simply who I am
outside of Christ. While my sins may trouble
me, God has made provision. I have only to say
my high priest's name, and His ever-flowing
blood touches the tarnished thread in the fabric
of my life and restores its luster. Faithful is He
as advocate, intercessor, and heavenly lawyer!

This is Jesus today!

ACKNOWLEDGMENTS

I want to thank Mike Morrell and Brittian Bullock for their editing efforts, Greg Daniel for supporting this project 150 percent, and the David C Cook team for turning the plain manuscript into an attractive volume. You all made this a much better book.

Get Frank Viola's New Online Discipleship Course!

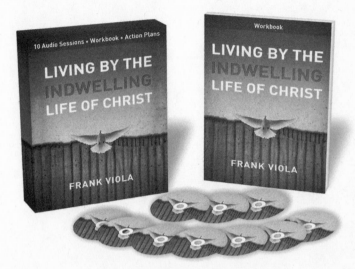

Living by the Indwelling Life of Christ is a ten-audio program with a practical workbook and bonus resources. Go to **TheDeeperJourney.com** for details and ordering information.